Order this book online at www.trafford.com
or email orders@trafford.com

Most Trafford titles are also available at major online book retailers.

Printed in the United States of America.

ISBN: 978-1-4269-4683-7 (sc)
ISBN: 978-1-4269-4684-4 (e)

*Our mission is to efficiently provide the world's finest, most comprehensive book publishing
service, enabling every author to experience success. To find out how to publish your
book, your way, and have it available worldwide, visit us online at www.trafford.com*

Trafford rev. 11/06/2010

 www.trafford.com

North America & international
toll-free: 1 888 232 4444 (USA & Canada)
phone: 250 383 6864 ♦ fax: 812 355 4082

Betrayal of the Beloved

By Ingrid Heller

Based on a true contemporary story

"Once upon
a time,
in the world
of adults,
the unexpected had to be expected.
Such is the drama of life where all
players
involved
are just
acting
their
role.
None
is more
important
than
the other.
None is better or worse than the other.
All that is happening, though perceived
as Good or Evil, is serving the highest Good."

CONTENTS

Dedicated to my family, friends and teachers.

MAIKA'S STORY UNVEILED

I WILL never forget the phone call from Maika on that late Friday night. I was stunned. I froze in fear of something like that happening to me. The guilt I felt the following week, that I couldn't make myself available to my dear friend and confidante over the years, haunted me. I failed her. She made herself available to me any time I needed her. I was the first one she called after she completed her emergency phone call to the police. They also failed her. No one was available. Maika told me her story in a nut shell with a shaken voice. I was in disbelief. "Is this real?" I asked.

It was real! That was the most frightening fact about the incident. It did happen and it could happen to any of us. I shrank for a while, remembering stories of abuses done to women. Maika asked me to come over. She pleaded with me.

"I am afraid to show up!" I told her. "I am sorry, but I don't have courage to come over. Isn't there someone else you could ask?"

I think Maika forgave me at that very moment. She understood. I phoned her a week later. She asked me to come over and I did this time. We have spent many hours on the phone since then. I made myself available. Her story was so rare, and perhaps more common than I thought, that we both agreed to share it. Maika didn't mind.

"It could help others to make better choices", she claimed.

Maika's case is an important story on many levels. It became a lesson, which only a few would ask for and understand.

Two years earlier, Maika bought a lovely house with a garden in a good neighbourhood. That house was just waiting for her to drive by and to notice the Open House sign on the main road, directing her into a pleasant and quiet cul-de-sac. She fell in love with it right away, and so did her boyfriend. She took her children to see it. They also liked it and its closeness to schools. The down payment manifested itself with short term loans from friends. She had friends. The offer was accepted. It was a good price for the property like that. There was nothing wrong with it. It had all imaginable features of today's modern homes. The vendor was building a family home in the suburbs and needed to sell. He listed it right after 9-11, the very number Maika phoned before she called me on that day.

Maika had only three months available to match the minimum down payment for the mortgage. She used what she applied most of her life – faith and trust. She felt very strongly that the house was there for her family. One of her daughters was a professional with good income. Maika asked her for help with the mortgage qualification and having no issues with trust, she offered to have her on the titles of the property. A trusted old friend matched the qualification and the loan was approved. Maika had a blessed season. Clients were pouring in and she was making money to collect the rest of the down payment. There was a moment when she gave in to worrying around Christmas time, but picked herself up again and made it. She was a renter up to then, concerned about the security of her home. The landlady was much over ninety and in poor health. Maika prayed for her, asking her soul to wait till she'd have her own roof over a head. When Maika moved into her new house, the next morning the son of the landlady called to say that his mother passed on that morning. She had waited till the day Maika slept in her own house with her family.

At times, I was amazed with the timing in Maika's life. She had more appointments during this season than ever before! She had enough funds to pay cash for renovations, legal fees, and household items and to repay her friends. Her professional daughter had an agreement with her mother. Maika was to pay every penny for whatever expense related to the purchase, ownership and the maintenance of the property. Her daughter and the trusted friend were on the titles. He held a proxy for Maika and they all agreed that the titles would be transferred to Maika's name as soon as possible.

Spring arrived. Maika and her boyfriend transformed the garden into a fertile field, surrounded by a charming rock garden. Friends were coming over for a beer and chat, all enjoying the beauty and quiet of the backyard. All of them were happy for Maika. At last, she had a home of her own. One friend suggested a roommate to help her with mortgage payments. Maika liked the idea, but then she and her children would lose privacy and her boyfriend might feel insecure. She declined the idea, but was open to it, just in case the right person would come along. Her boyfriend had young children yet and was not ready to move in, or to help out.

Summer came. Vegetables in the garden grew to oversize, as if a magic wand raised them from the ground. Maika just smiled when any of us complimented on her green thumb, directing our attention to many plastic devas and faeries she positioned around the rock garden. "They watch over; I gave them the assignment", she replied each time. The harvest was amazing. She had plenty for all of us.

Autumn leaves covered the garden, then got buried in the turned soil, and the winter set in. It was not a very good winter – it was long and cold. The Iraq war was on the horizon and everyone began to wonder what is going to happen with the economy. Those who knew about war economies did not worry. Most people watched their money and hardly any clients phoned. Maika paid her mortgage weekly. I could feel the stress she had. She sometimes phoned me just a day before her mortgage payment was due, "God loves me! I made it again! I have money for the payment!" I think God had loved her all the time. She always made it, barely, but made it. I would freak, but Maika has seldom shown stress or concern over money. I observed that providence was on her side. Sometimes I wondered if she really had faith and trust, or was she simply an irresponsible adult. My own ancestors had their share of struggle in life; I was not the type that would voluntarily enter the situation Maika has chosen, though we both had a very similar philosophy of life that we reap what we create, which taught us to be good people and do our best. We only made different choices. I believed in choosing thoughtfully and intelligently, learning from the past and practicing caution, while Maika just threw herself into all kinds of situations, because her emotional quotient was high and ruled in her life. She refused to delve on negative experiences, as if the past didn't exist in her world. I liked my own comfort, some predictability, and always have welcomed the magic of each day, those so called coincidences and synchronicities that reminded me about the wholeness of the universe and the consciousness in everything that is. Maika was more of a researcher and adventurer, testing the laws of nature, experimenting with cause and effect, and witnessing directly in her life affairs how consciousness is operating in our lives. She loved life!

CHOICES

IT was close to the beginning of the Iraq war, when the world froze and started another cycle of facing its own karma. The aggressor tried to justify its action, and the victim had its reaction. The time of deception entered our existence and none of us was spared. Some were able to face a greater darkness and release it to the light; others just observed and hoped to understand.

Around this time, Maika became a grandmother. She was thrilled. She waited for this little brave soul that has been expected for several years now. Maika gave up on childbearing idea when she was forty-seven, though she had a strong feeling that one more child wanted to be born to her. He came through her daughter, living eleven hundred kilometers away. Maika was able to cope with her immediate expenses with a small short term loan from a friend, but there was no money left for the grandson's gift, or for a visit. This time timing was not on her side. She contemplated something she would have never expected to happen. She decided to sell her house, to the amazement of all of us. "Why?" we all asked. "I have to", she replied. "It will solve all my problems. I will start all over again. I have only one child at home now and he is already working. He can live on his own. I need to reorganize my life. Come on, I can do it at this age! I had many starts; I am good at it by now!" she kept on reminding our long and speechless faces. Then we became concerned regarding her practice – her livelihood, "Where will you work from?" As usual, she had a solution "I can go mobile. And I need a break and do something else for a while." We have accepted and respected her choice. This very decision of hers started another cycle of an unusual timing of events.

Maika has consulted a realtor friend about the listing of her property. He offered to do it for a greatly reduced commission. The boyfriend kept on reminding Maika to transfer the titles to her name prior to the sale.

"I have a feeling in my gut that you alone should be on the titles of the property."

It was a comment he couldn't resist. He made Maika react the way only a mother would have.

"Are you telling me that I cannot trust my own child?"

"Not at all, but you just never know! She doesn't like me and has opposed our relationship since I've met her. She offered to pay for the transaction, hasn't she?"

"But that was before I thought of selling, sweetie. Now we will leave it to the moment of sale. Don't worry. All will be well."

The boyfriend did worry regardless, but chose to stay out of it and do his best. He offered Maika a trip to see her grandson. That made her very happy. As a matter of fact, that very same night she went to check out the prices of baby clothes. The trip was planned for the 21st day of the child's age.

The realtor friend was encouraging Maika to list the property prior to the trip. She had almost agreed to it, but another male friend had the most unusual proposition for her. When he found out that she was going to sell the house in this lovely neighbourhood, he offered to buy a half of it.

"A half of the house? How? And why?" Maika asked in disbelief.

Brad was a well-educated man having a good working position with the government agency in environmental sciences. He knew Maika from dance classes. There he found out about her intention to sell her property. When she mentioned a sale of her house, a very warm feeling came over him. Right then he spontaneously offered to co-own the house with her. They didn't know each other well. They just liked each other. He was single, still unmarried in his forties, a handsome and well-mannered man, and he had some common interests with her. Maika saw

Brad's offer as a gift presented by Providence, a solution to her problem. He would pay her a half of the equity, which would cover for more than her present debts, and they would share a financial responsibility related to the property, and likely would share a residence. Each time she sat in her living room and observed the spacious hardwood floor area, she wondered who would dance there with her. Dancing alone and without a partner wasn't much fun. Her boyfriend didn't feel confident about his dancing, though, sometimes they practiced together. And here she was, sitting right across the dancer's chair and who was asking her to view her home with the intention of buying a half of it.

"Brad, I will give you a call toward the end of the week. That will give you enough time to change your mind. Look, your offer is unusual. Are you sure you know what you are propositioning?"

Brad just smiled. He was still radiant.

"I feel that I am doing the right thing. I have this beautiful fuzzy feeling inside me since the idea came over me. Call me, Maika!", and he sealed a little kiss onto her cheek, pressing a business card into her hand.

There was no need to explain anything to Maika. She was sure that the Universe interjected and wanted her to stay in the house. She phoned her friends about it. They all said that Brad is an answer to her problem and that she can continue enjoying her home and continue with her home-based practice.

Maika told her boyfriend about the offer. That didn't go well. He was skeptical and wondered about Brad's motivation. He posed many questions about Brad. In reality, it all boiled down to his concern about the impact such a partnership would have on their relationship and the privacy they had so far. Maika realized herself that it would be challenging to keep harmony and peace with Frank, while having a male roommate. She loved Frank and he was an important person in her life. They have known and dated each other for over two years now and hoped to create a future together. Right now, they couldn't commit in the conjugal relationship, but the day was coming and they both believed that they had better potential as a couple than most. Some of Maika's friends liked Frank, others wondered and felt that she was giving him a chunk of her life, considering her age. Her youngest son also liked him, especially when he stayed over for a weekend and helped out with chores. They were like a family on those days.

Brad came to see the property. He loved it! He asked Maika what her friends were saying about the possible partnership they would create. Brad admitted that all his friends were trying to talk him out of it, but he was sure himself that he was making the right choice.

They sat down in the living room. Brad looked around and imagined himself living there, dancing on the spacious hardwood floor. He did not neglect to compliment Maika on her homemaking.

"Beautiful plants you got, Maika!"

"I love plants, and the garden here. It is a part of my world; there is lots of 'me' in this place", she added, while she was gathering courage to tell him what was on her mind.

"Brad, I am not sure that taking you as a partner in the ownership of the house will be fair toward you."

"What makes you say that, Maika?" asked Brad, somewhat confused.

"You see, if I sell the entire property to someone, I will have a total freedom to start in the place of my choice. If in partnership, and I would walk away from the partnership later on, I would not have much left. Yes, my expenses would be cut in half till then, but ... very often the equity of the property is the only sum of money we are able to accumulate. I don't want any of us to be losers, Brad."

Brad appreciated Maika's concern and decided to give her more time to reconsider, but he assured her that regardless of her doubts, he still wanted to seal the deal. All this time he was peaceful and feeling comfortable with his decision.

He repeated himself again, "I know, Maika that I am supposed to do this. It gives me the most wonderful and sweet feeling I don't remember having, ever. Now I see you in your beautiful home, and how passionately you spoke of your garden to me, and also seeing that it is the place of your work, I feel even stronger about my proposition to you. And your son could continue living with you!"

Maika loved her children and she often expressed a concern how she'll be able to cope when her youngest one leaves home. He was doing an apprenticeship as a chef in a downtown restaurant, something he wanted to do for some time. Maika often picked him up in the late night hours, or after midnight to drive him home. That way she had peace of mind that he was safe. The city was experiencing increasing crime, so typical for large cities.

"Brad, I will give it a serious thought again. I will not list the house with the realtor yet. This needs to be given a chance."

Brad was relieved and assured Maika that she would not regret it. Her son came home at this very moment and had a short chat with Brad. They had chemistry. Allan was taking his career seriously, and yet, he managed to have some fun times with friends he had since junior high. He was a nice and sociable lad.

The following day a client called for the appointment. Though it was Sunday, Maika made herself available. She needed the money for gifts. When she walked downstairs to her office with him, she had a feeling that the carpeting was spongy. When the client left, she checked the utility room. One hot water tank had a leak and the water was seeping under the wall into her office. A plumber friend came over, sealed the leak and helped Maika to remove the bookcases from the office. Indeed, there was a soaked underlay and the top carpet was already getting wet. It took Maika one week to dry it all out and make it look like new again. Then her trip to see her grandson was nearing. The realtor phoned about the listing. Maika asked him to phone her in two weeks. She told him about the leak. He had news for her about the house two streets down that sold within twenty-four hours, having less features than Maika's, at the price she originally hoped to get for hers. She phoned Brad and promised to give him a final answer when she'll be back in four days. She also phoned her daughter and the friend who had titles on her house, telling them about the option she had and that she would decide either way on her way back.

When Maika held her grandson in her arms and observed his peaceful face, she was reminded of our individual importance and of our place in the world. What is his Journey going to be like? He entered this world with trust that adults can seldom reclaim. His calm facial expression had become an image of encouragement for months to come in his grandmother's life, a true gift from an infant like himself: to practice acceptance and to trust.

TO HAVE OR NOT TO HAVE

MAIKA desired to move forward with a clean shield. She was well aware that its reflection might mirror and intensify the outer image of the world with its players in the drama of life. She was willing to surface the issues remaining in her energy field that were waiting and resting unresolved. Just a little ripple of action would stir a reaction. Neither of us knew what it was, or when it was coming.

I remembered one lovely visit at Maika's garden patio, while we enjoyed refreshing orange juice flavoured by floating fresh mint leaves, when she stared into her glass, as if it turned into a crystal ball. She paused for a while. I noticed concern in her features, confirmed by her words "Bonnie, there is something that bothers me. I have stability in my life now. Business is good, all worked out the way I would dreamed it. Externally all is calm."

"It was about time! Don't you think that you deserve that?" I asked.

"It is not about that, Bonnie. When there is too much calm on the outside, there is great activity on the inside, even without our awareness. You know, like before the storm, all is very calm, suddenly", she was looking for right words, "I am speaking of cycles, life's breathing, in and out, a contraction before the birth of some big event."

"Maika, enjoy what is now. Don't worry about what may or may not be coming."

"I just hope it is not going to be too much to handle. Life is too good right now," and she paused for another moment, "I wouldn't want to move again. It is a good family place. My daughter is expecting, did I tell you that?" All of a sudden she lit up.

"Yes, you told me that you were going to be a grandmother. How is Lucy?"

We talked about our families, reflecting on years of our struggles and joys.

Children were very important to Maika. She was one of those mothers who devoted many years to rearing them, enrolling them in good schools, driving them both ways daily and in her spare time she prepared their food rich in nutrients or contacted potential clients to earn some money for basic needs. Their home was always neat and comfortable. She always said with a smile "that it was her most important job and the only job without pay". Not everyone noticed that she lacked money. She was resourceful and very organized, despite their empty fridge on most days. Her children ate food made from scratch and it showed in their healthy physique and clever minds.

Brad phoned Maika on the day of her arrival home. "How was your trip?" he asked. "How is your grandson?"

"He is so handsome, Brad! He inspired me with courage."

"Are we going to sign a deal, then? Is the first of May as a possession day fine with you?" Brad sincerely hoped to reach an agreement with Maika.

"Brad, I hope I won't regret my decision."

"I assure you that you won't be disappointed with me. We can insert all details into our contract, if you wish. I know that I am doing the right thing and truly, I'd like to see you continuing with your practice. Maybe there was a void in the economy for a while, but it is going to pick up again, you'll see." Brad sounded very positive and confident. He was well informed by then about the holders of the titles, the necessary transfers and his realtor had appraised the house at the same price as she would list for. Brad was ready to pay thirty thousand dollars for his equity share and thus liberate Maika from her debts and provide her with lovely savings, to which she could add more every month.

Maika's answer was unexpected. All of us, her friends, hoped that she would accept Brad's offer. On one hand, we had selfish reasons, such as visiting and enjoying her place, dinner parties with great conversations, but those of us who met Brad, hoped that the two of them would get closer and tie the knot eventually. Frank was not the type we wanted to see in her life. But, how can we tell a friend we care about? We learned to accept him. None of us sees into the future. We could only see the immediate good and a solution to her existing problem.

"Brad, I will list with a realtor tomorrow."

Brad had little to say. He also was respectful of other people's free will.

"Just in case you changed your mind, Maika, let me know toward the end of April. You can always cancel the listing."

"I don't want you to be stuck because of me and this house, Brad. Now the prices of real estate are pretty high, but we don't know where it will lead in the future. Just imagine if it stays about the same, or gets lower. The dollar is pretty unstable compared to the Euro. No matter what would be happening in our personal lives, we would have to stay here. If I chose to leave, I might be without resources. Believe me, Brad, it is not an easy decision. It is about 'to have, or not to have' for both of us. I already told you a number of times that your offer is appreciated."

Brad recognized that Maika was serious about her decision. He honoured her choice, but stressed again his intention. At this point, Maika also responded to her emotions. She hoped to visit her baby grandson often, her elderly mother needed her, and Maika needed a Sabbatical for a few months – all so enticing to her free-spirited nature that she really embodied and needed to express.

Frank and the realtor were likely the only individuals who welcomed Maika's decision. Clients were concerned with their own interest in mind, while her youngest son Allan was daydreaming about renting a downtown apartment on his own, close to his workplace. Frank kept on reminding Maika about the change of names on the titles, while the realtor and other parties involved were willing to wait for the moment of sale. The house was ready to be shown toward the end of March on days of heavy snowfall.

TIMING

THE snow remained on the ground this time and the temperatures dropped far below the freezing point. The world was still and only a few clients phoned Maika for appointments. Lucy, her eldest daughter called. She wanted to know if she could cash a gift cheque Maika gave her for a baby stroller.

"Of course, you could!" was Maika's reply.

Maika would seldom show her lack. The amount on the cheque equalled her weekly mortgage payment.

"Will you be okay without this money, Mom?" asked her concerned daughter.

"I am always okay. Even if I had nothing left in the account after that, the money will quickly come in. I have appointments booked; I will be fine. Just go ahead and cash it!" Maika's voice was reassuring. She never doubted Providence.

Most of her friends, me included, admired this quality Maika possessed. She had the trust of a child.

Her eldest son called and asked Maika for a favour. He needed to stay a month at Maika's place. His lease was expiring and he had to move at the end of April. Ron needed to accumulate enough money to lease a place starting in June. He asked to stay at Maika's for the month of May.

"Son, it is not a good time for that," she explained. "I have the house up for sale; realtors are bringing their clients at any time of day. The house must always be clean and organized. You are a messy boy, working shifts and sleeping in the morning. I get phone calls during the day and must get a good night's sleep. I am afraid that I cannot help you this time."

"Mom, please ...... I will be clean....." Ron did not give up.

"You? Clean? People don't change that fast. Ask some of your friends. I am sure they can put you up for one month."

Ron came the next morning to shovel the snow of Maika's spacious driveway and all around the house. She was very appreciative. She called me that day and confided her thoughts in me.

"Do you think I am too hard on him?" she asked.

"Well, it is up to you, Maika. You can choose to rescue him again, or let him learn to be more responsible. What if he won't move out? Have you thought about that?"

"Why wouldn't he move out? The house will be sold. He will have to move out!"

At this point I decided to remind her of the years passed, when he was regularly coming over to borrow twenty dollars for gas or pocket money. He never paid it back. He borrowed larger sums of money from his younger siblings. They usually forgave the debt under the pretence of a birthday or Christmas gift. In early January of the year 2000 I phoned Maika and asked about her millennium and how she celebrated the New Year. She said that it was the worst one of her life. Ron came over New Year's Eve afternoon. He was the only child of hers who dared to go into her fridge and help himself. None of the other children would do that. Allan told his brother several times that he came over only to empty the fridge and borrow more money. Maika asked Ron about something he had done in the past and caused her a debt close to three thousand dollars. She reminded him that she wanted to leave this kind of practice behind and start fresh and clean into the new millennium. In that instant Ron said something to her that sounded close to "you deserved it" and he laughed into her face. She ordered him to leave. He would not. She pushed him out of her home; she against the strong six foot giant! As she attempted to direct him out with her body, he grabbed her hands and crushed them. Allan couldn't protect his mother. The older brother always bullied him and he was afraid of him, locking himself in his bedroom now. The terrible pain that Maika had to endure was only surpassed by her courage to stand up to her son's abuses. She threw his boots out the door and he had to leave. He phoned half an hour later. He called her "psycho" and "out of touch". Her hands were swollen, painful and weak. It took nearly a month to be free of pain during simple household chores. She needed her hands to earn a living, do chores and clear the snow. If the police had not been as busy on that day, ready for Y2K, she would have called. She had no car at this time and even if she had, she could not steer the wheel with her injured hands. This was the greatest assault on her motherhood. Her good friends Nick and Bobbie assisted her psychologically and tried to heal the wound. "We live in unprecedented times", they both said. "Young people are given all kinds of weapons against parents. Have you heard of children taking their parents to court? We've lost authority; it was taken from us by existing laws!" For a moment I thought of reminding Maika of this incident, but then I admired her capacity to forgive and forget and decided to approach it from another angle.

"Maika, you asked my opinion about Ron moving in ... well, my response is simple. Don't take him in. He cannot be trusted."

Maika confessed that other friends also advised her the same way. Frank literally froze in his features, when she told him about Ron's request. Frank had no idea what happened on the Y2K night. She never told him – she was ashamed. There were only three or four of us who knew. Other friends just wondered why she cut all communication with Ron and why he could only visit for Christmas dinner, when two of his siblings and Maika's ex-husband were there. She could be at peace in their company. Ron brought gifts for everyone that time. He had a good job and treated the family to many goodies that Maika could not afford.

"I think he has changed, Bonnie. He has learned his lessons. I could use the money he'd pay me for the month's rent for one mortgage payment!"

"I sure expect you to charge him! If I were you, Maika, I would not take him in. He is not very respectful, as you well know. Don't do anything you would regret later on!"

A mother's dilemma is about love for her offspring - love that is seldom reciprocated. It is taken for granted. It is considered a part of motherhood. Nature made mothers that way. They just give from the heart; they always forgive and forget the injustice done to them. Such is love.

Against all warnings, Maika allowed her son to move his many boxes, some pieces of furniture and his uninsured car into her garage, parking her own vehicle on the street. We, her friends, hoped it would be only that. Then her daughter needed help with the baby and Maika began to plan for the trip. Frank was somewhat aware of her financial situation and offered to pay for the trip. He actually encouraged her to take three days for herself and join him on his trip to the coast in his camper van. They'd stop in the hot springs on the way and camp. He had relatives in Vancouver he hadn't visited for some time. The trip was scheduled for Sunday, but Frank wanted to leave on Friday, the day when Maika made her regular weekly mortgage payments.

Brad called around this time and asked Maika one more time about her decision. She told him that her son needed a place and Brad considered taking him in for one month. Brad had one room in his house vacant at this time. Ron came over to his mom's instead and asked if he could pay his rent share on the last day of April. Maika emphasized that it must be on that day at the latest, since her mortgage payment was due the following day and she must have her finances in order prior to the trip. Ron said that he would move in till he pays. Maika prepared one room for his stay. She also paid all the outstanding bills before she travelled. Ron's payment would cover for the mortgage and she'd be back early enough to earn money for the next mortgage payment due. She had a post-dated cheque from one client already. All was well and she could travel on Friday morning, on the first day of May.

In the evening before the trip, she phoned Eva, the daughter who had her name on the titles and on whose name was the mortgage loan and account to which payments were made. Maika told her that she was going to visit her nephew and sister and that she'll make the payment in the morning with Ron's rent money.

Eva was disturbed hearing about her brother staying with her mother.

"Are you sure he'll pay you, Mom? You know how he is!"

"He'll give me the money tonight, he said. He is also getting his damage deposit back. He'll pay me. Otherwise, he cannot stay here."

Eva was restless; she felt uncomfortable about the news.

"You didn't pass him the keys yet, did you?"

"He slept here last night and tonight will pay me. He actually was going to stay overnight in his other place, but I let him sleep here. At first he said he'll sleep here after he pays."

Eva was primarily concerned about the mortgage payment. She had her accounts tied in together; one would cover for the other. She was a high income earner and had no real reason to worry about money. The house would sell soon. Eva just wanted to get out of the mortgage loan commitment and see her mother free of a heavy financial burden. She herself noticed that the last year was hard on her, compared to the more prosperous previous years.

Some friends analyzed Maika's situation from a more spiritual angle. Nick reminded her several times that she's been having financial challenges since she committed to Frank. "He's got a lack in his aura, Maika! You're taking on your lover's stuff. He also takes too much of your time, while you could generate more income. Don't give your power away like that!"

Maika paid attention to what her friends were saying, but rarely heeded their advice. Nick also did not want her to assist Ron with housing, especially at this time when she wanted to sell. "What if he takes advantage of you?" he said. He also recommended her to transfer the titles to her name, but knowing both the trusted friend as proxy on the titles and Eva, he relaxed and let go.

Ron came home late the night before the trip. Maika instructed Allan to deposit Ron's payment into the account, providing the bank card and wrote down the PIN. He was very nervous about it.

"What if he doesn't pay me and I cannot help you, Mom?"

"He will likely pay me in the morning. This is just in a case of a delay. Eva will take care of the debit otherwise."

Frank arrived on time in the morning. Maika decided to wake Ron up, asking him for the rent money. His answer surprised her.

"You're taking advantage of me," he said with a sleepy and irritating voice.

"Ron, I need it to make a mortgage payment! It is due today and so is your rent! I have to leave soon!"

"That's your problem," replied Ron. "I don't have money on me now. I will pass it to Allan later."

Maika had no choice, but to trust. If she had suspected this, she would have waited with the other bill payments. They were not overdue yet.

Frank witnessed the dialogue and began to worry. He never had a chance to get to know Eva and Ron. He sensed that they didn't like him. His status didn't appeal to Maika's older children. He was only comfortable and had to provide for his own children yet. Eva liked when her mom dated a well-educated and well-to-do men. When she found out that she was dating Frank, she insisted that she'd stop seeing him.

"He isn't good for you, Mom. He's got too many issues, too much baggage. Break up with him before you fall in love again!" were Eva's exact words.

It was already too late then. Maika was in love. Brad's partnership would have doubtlessly disturbed her relationship with Frank. Maika knew that she was entering uncertainty, leaving her quite prosperous practice behind, her clients, her livelihood. She trusted that the Universe had something greater ready for her. Frank, on the contrary, liked predictability. Maika's lifestyle didn't appeal to him. He tried hard not to talk about his concerns, but sometimes it just slipped out of his mouth. Maika only replied, "It is not for everyone. You must feel connected and loved. I had no real spouse to partner with. I had only a soul to rely on, my all-knowing twin."

WARNING SIGNS

THE westbound highway was clear. The trees in the Columbia River Valley, veiled in a light green colour, announced the arrival of spring. The first night stay was at the Halcyon Hot Springs near Revelstoke - Maika's favourite destination. The dip in the mineral rich pool treated with ozone was the perfect prescription for Maika. She recharged her body for days to come when she'd care for her grandson and help with the household, so her daughter could have a good sleep, for a change.

Frank enjoyed Maika's company. He took this time off his work, a kind of short holiday, to help her out with the trip. He needed to be back for the following Friday night. He promised his children to take them skiing on Saturday – the last ski trip of the season. Maika appreciated his commitment. She could speak with him almost about anything, except the spiritual dimensions of life. He couldn't see the greater picture leading to life's events, but he was a great listener. He loved hearing about Maika's adventures in the past and now about her grandson. She was the first grandmother he had ever dated and the craziest one too, as he claimed. She made him laugh each time her observations of life reached beyond the boundaries of his perception. She could find humour and beauty in things others seldom noticed. He liked to view the world through her rose glasses! He just could not fully accept her way of dealing with life's challenges. He fully refrained from offering advice, except the one about the titles. He welcomed that she did not accept Brad's offer. Actually, he thought the offer was suspicious and felt that Brad had a personal interest in Maika. Frank found her very attractive and sexy and was not surprised when others would feel the same way about her. Now, she was entirely with him in her favourite environment amidst the pristine nature by the lake. Relaxed and content, she immersed herself totally in the feeling of being loved and protected.

A nightmare woke up Maika toward the morning. Frank noticed her awkward breathing and became concerned, but Maika would not share with him the dream she had. She chose to keep it to herself. During the morning she analyzed it in her mind. There could not be a clearer message than the story of her dream. It disturbed her. She knew only one way – moving toward the future and facing it fearlessly.

A long drive ahead seemed much shorter in Frank's company. They chatted, sang together, listened to some music, while enjoying the beautiful scenery of British Columbia. Finally, when they reached her destination, they sadly parted to be reunited again in four days. Frank was to pick her up early Thursday morning for their trip back home, with an overnight stay near the hot springs again.

Maika used all her time to help out with the baby, cooking, baking and other chores. She loved doing that! The little one slept soundly for hours when she laid him in his crib and toward the morning, when he was waking up, she fed him, changed his diaper and took him to her bed, keeping him on her chest. Her own babies loved that! They were calmed by Mom's heartbeat and enjoyed the perfect warmth. Now, she was bonding to the next generation. There was harmony ....until an early evening phone call. It was from Eva, who was obviously upset. In her loud voice she asked her mother why she counted on Ron and let her down.

"If you don't deposit that money to the account by Tuesday, I will close the account!" she stated in a superior commanding voice.

"I don't want to be yelled at", responded Maika and hung up the receiver.

Within seconds, Eva called back. Lucy picked it up again and spoke to her for a moment, passing the receiver to Maika, with a sarcastic smile.

Another session of shouting followed, all about the promise and commitment Maika took on when asking Eva for the mortgage qualification and that now the agreement was broken.

"Eva, cover for it in the meanwhile and I will straighten this out with you when I get back. I cannot do anything from here. I don't even have my bank card with me. Call Ron and ask him for the money."

"What do you think I did?! He just laughed! You shouldn't have trusted him! I can't believe you did that! I bet he is smoking in that house!"

Eva would have continued with her loud and upset voice, if Maika had not interjected.

"Do what you think is right. I will phone the guys right away."

Maika called home, but no one answered. She left a message, asking her youngest son to call her.

That evening Maika reviewed the dream she had on Friday night. Was Ron plotting to cheat her after all? The young man in the dream could very well be her son!

Maika wished Frank would call. She needed to talk this over with someone outside her immediate family and close to her heart, someone who cared and would understand. Frank asked her a couple of times on their way to the coast about Ron. "Do you think he'll pay you, Maika?" She always replied that he would. Maybe if she expressed some doubt, Frank would rather have loaned her the money.

Maika began to regret her decision to assist Ron. He had a streak in him that couldn't be trusted. He was a smooth talker, clever and quick with his mind. For some time Maika didn't know who his friends were. The old friends seemed to perish and new ones were appearing. Ron had left her home nine years ago. He was self-made by now. Ron was hoping to find investors for his new business idea. He had a nicely drafted business plan and researched quite thoroughly the competition. It looked promising for him.

Maika succeeded in reaching Allan that night. He said that Ron had not paid him yet and when asked to remind him, he was reluctant. Maika acknowledged that he was afraid of dealing with his brother. But he agreed to ask Ron to call her at Lucy's place.

Ron called the next day in the late afternoon. When Maika asked him about his rent overdue, he replied that he was not going to pay her for the next two weeks. He needed to wait for his damage deposit refund from the previous residence. "I told you so!" he stressed.

Suddenly Maika remembered the three phone calls on Thursday morning. The callers asked for Ron and wouldn't leave a message. Maika had a feeling that they were personal creditors. She recognized one caller, but he was brief and would not respond to her "How are you? It's so nice to hear your voice!" He used to be Ron's friend for years and spent one Christmas with Maika's family. Now she was sure that one damage deposit refund was to be shared with a number of people.

"Ron, I want you to move out of my house by Friday! You lied to me!"

Ron laughed hysterically, while replying, "It is you who will move out, if anyone! I have no intention to leave. I am here and you're not!"

At this moment Maika lost it. "You, you are such a disgrace! How glad I am that you don't carry my name!" She was beside herself, raising her voice, as if her words could not be heard otherwise.

That gave Ron greater power. He laughed even more now and asked if Frank heard her speaking this way and stated "I will make sure Frank leaves you!" The tone of his voice came from the abyss itself, as sly and disgusting as it was.

"By Friday you'll be out of there!" Maika trembled while she entered the room where Lucy sat with the baby in her arms.

Now Lucy raised her voice. "I don't want you to yell like that here! I don't like it and my son doesn't deserve it!"

Lucy had a point. Maika attempted to explain what happened, but Lucy cut her off. "I don't want to hear about it! It is your fault that you let him move in. You know how he is!"

Maika was in tears. "That boy has caused me so much pain! I will never come to his wedding, nor invite him for Christmas! As far as I am concerned, he is not my son anymore!"

"Yes, he is your son, Mother and you still have to face him. He is living in your house and you don't right now!"

Lucy distanced herself from her mother that same evening. Whatever Maika did for Lucy and her family from then on, wasn't good enough. Lucy's husband returned from his business trip the following day and took care of his son at night. Maika and Lucy could have an uninterrupted sleep that way, but Maika couldn't rest her mind anymore. She kept on trying to reach her friend Jeff, who was proxy on the titles, but he was at the Trade Show and she could not remember his cell number. She could not remember other numbers either, as stressed as she was. She needed to contact someone urgently who could phone Jeff's home and ask for the number. Then she remembered a phone number of her former boyfriend. He quickly responded and offered assistance. He knew about Ron's past. He became very concerned. Maika pleaded with him to contact Allan and make sure that he was not harassed by his brother. That was too much to ask. She was promised a cell phone number. She received it the next day. She was only able to leave a message for Jeff. No one called back. She called his office number and left another message with a brief explanation, asking Jeff's permission to change locks on her house. Legally, she was not the owner of her own house. She wished she had listened to Frank. He must have sensed something only an outsider could have perceived. Maika was the insider. In hope that she would hear from Frank earlier, she was able to rest a little. Ironically, that day was Ron's birthday. She was not up to calling her son. Just twenty-eight years ago he was as sweet as her grandson was now. He also slept on his mother's chest. Maika's grandmother said once: "When the children are babies, they suck their mother's milk. When they are adults, they suck her blood." That was her response to Maika's choice of having more children.

Frank called on Wednesday afternoon. He wanted to leave earlier. He said that he felt they should be on their way back. Lucy reminded Maika of her promise to watch over the little one that night. She planned on going out with her husband. Maika told Frank that they should leave in the morning instead. Nothing else was mentioned. Frank asked about her time with the family and she answered only to that. There was no privacy to talk about anything else. She just said that she had a lot to share with him. He took it on a positive note. Maika actually looked forward to having a private time with her grandson. She had not sung to him yet, nor told him the story of his descent to the Earth, to unite with those he had always loved.

HAPPY MOTHER'S DAY

LUCY had a thoughtful Mother's Day gift ready for her Mom. Maika parted with everyone when Frank arrived. Lucy had met him in March at the airport. He took a few pictures of Maika's family now and rushed to his camper van.

Maika waited with her story until the heavy morning traffic passed. When they were arriving near Abbotsford, she told Frank what had happened. He listened very carefully, showing signs of concern.

"Maika, I had a feeling that Ron came to you with another intention. He needs money for his business. He might blackmail you! You are a source for him!"

"Frank, if I had a suspecting mind, I would think that too. He is my son! How can I mistrust my own flesh and blood?"

"He is also someone else's child, don't forget that!"

Maika paused for a while, going into memories of previous years.

"When his father died, those kids changed. Sometimes, I couldn't recognize them! They acted like him!"

"Eva is also his child, isn't she?" Frank looked very serious.

"Lucy, Ron and Eva are his children."

"How is Allan getting along with them?"

"Girls love him, but Ron had issues. He bullied him, called him a 'spoiled brat' and yet kept on borrowing money from him, never paying back. Allan is saving his allowance from his Dad and spends money wisely. True, I could afford buying more for Allan than the others. He is a good lad; polite, sensitive and appreciative. Good manners are natural to him. People like him."

"Sweetie, I am glad you have him," and squeezed Maika's hand lovingly to seal his words.

It was not easy to let go of all kinds of thoughts and concerns. Sometimes the conversation took a twist into all kinds of speculations, but that was exactly the time when Frank asked Maika to sing for him. Music took her to better places, to the never-never land of her dreams.

They stopped at the same hot springs place and camped overnight in a nearby campground. Right there Frank asked Maika about the dream she had six days earlier in that area. This time, Maika was anxious to tell him.

"It was a short dream, really. It was a very uncomfortable dream. I will describe it in words that are fitting the event: I am standing against a one meter high concrete wall that looked like a foundation. I had my hands on it - the wall supported me. Both my feet were a step away from the wall. I couldn't detach from the wall; I was stuck in that position. I wore a dress. I couldn't move in the dream. Neither could I turn my head – I could only look ahead. A male figure thrusts himself three times against me from behind. He screwed me behind my back! I felt very appalled, yet could do nothing. Then he just walked away by my left side. He chose a left hand path. I saw a young and naked male, who looked at me over his shoulder with ravish while walking away. He seemed desperate and yet repulsed by his own act."

"Who do you think he was, Maika?"

"Now I know that he was my son, Ron. Awful, isn't it?!"

"Why didn't you tell me about the dream? I would have turned back and dealt with it! Lucy could have looked after her baby on her own for a few more days! Whose idea was it to come over?"

"We both decided. She was exhausted. She is overly diligent and organized, everything must be according to a schedule and she doesn't know how to relax yet. Her husband was to be away and I really wanted to see that little one again. Remember, I wanted to leave on Sunday, but you rushed it for Friday."

"Oh, Maika, Maika, Maika! What if Ron is still there? What will you do then?"

Frank was very worried. He had a previous commitment with his children and could not stay at Maika's to assist with the situation.

"We'll arrive on time. Ron is working evenings now. I will have the locks changed before he comes from work. I know a locksmith who'll do it for me. I only worry about Allan."

In reality, Maika worried about more than that. She even thought of the amount on the gift cheque to Lucy, the exact amount of money she was short of. She wondered if she would have let Ron move in if she had broken even. Brad appeared to save her from this situation. He described the feeling he had when he offered Maika a partnership. It was a gift from the Universe. She had choices. She chose the hard way, without recognizing the signs. Behind the virtues of fairness and compassion, deception and malice were hiding in their shadows.

Upon arrival, Maika and Frank anxiously entered the house. Maika rushed to Ron's room. It was locked. He had a new lock put on his door. The kitchen was messy, with dishes unwashed. She noticed three business cards from realtors on the table who had brought their clients. She felt embarrassed about the state of her home. Then she rushed downstairs and asked Frank to help her to take Ron's desk and computer out into the garage. The garage had a new lock too. She phoned a locksmith friend. He was on his way to do a three-hour job for his best client. She begged him to come to her house first. He was upset about her lack of understanding. When Maika told him that it was a matter of life and death, he asked about her panic and the urgency. Maika quickly explained, but he responded, "What? He is your son!"

"That makes it even more dangerous. I need my front and back door locks changed and have you to open Ron's room and the garage. Please, help me!"

He promised and arrived within fifteen minutes. That kind of guy he was!

He opened the garage door and made her new keys for the lock. He did the same with Ron's room. Then he changed both locks on the front and back door and provided extra keys. He would not take a payment.

"You have enough on your plate now", he said. "Accept this from me, please. I was glad to help."

Maika knew that this good deed would be repaid to her special locksmith friend manifold.

Frank witnessed a disaster in Ron's room. The blinds and shutters were closed. There were cups of unfinished moldy coffee, cigarette buds floating in cups, and there was a cigarette smoke hanging in the air. It looked like a mad place. Frank helped Maika to take a large dresser out and left. Before that he was visibly shaken. He said that he had to get ready for tomorrow's skiing trip with his children and that he would call her on their return. Maika collected all her strength and began to take out all Ron's belongings. She placed most of the clothing into large suitcases she had and dragged it to the backyard. She hoped to be able to place it into the garage, but the door was blocked with heavy furniture and only some items could be placed in through a narrow opening. She could reach the garage door switch. It wouldn't open the door. Ron disconnected the cable. The remote opener was useless. Maika packed Ron's stuff in a roofed area by the garage inside the backyard and covered it with sheets. It was well protected. Then she rushed inside the house, secured all doors and windows, rolled down the outdoor roller shutters and typed and printed an Eviction Notice addressed to Ron, which she taped on both doors. Then she just waited.

The phone rang. She didn't dare to pick it up and waited for a few minutes. She checked the message. It was from Ron.

"Mother, I am coming home now. I want you to know that if you touch me, I will have the police involved. I have signed the lease with Eva, who is the owner of the house and she will sell the house for a price that she decides. I am sorry to tell you this, but you will end up with much less money than you anticipated. You can move out, or stay in the house – that is up to you. But, I am the principal tenant now and I set the rules. You can do absolutely nothing about that. Your rules don't apply anymore – the world is not running according to you. By the way, Happy Birthday to me!" he sang himself the famous tune and added, "Happy Mother's Day to you, ha-ha!" He laughed sarcastically.

Maika trembled. So, this is why her son needed the emergency roof over his head! He premeditated this! Now she knew why her friends warned her about Ron. She listened to the tape again and decided to record it. Her friends, to their shock, heard Ron's message later on.

Now Maika didn't hesitate and phoned 911 about the possible domestic conflict. The female operator refused to do anything.

"Ma'am, we have more urgent matters than yours. We have traffic accidents, murders, robberies, gang crime. Our cruisers are busy. Your claim is based on your fear. When your son assaults you, call us!"

Maika would not give up. "I took all precautions not to have him to break in, but there are windows without shutters and he could get in. There is a history of violence with him."

"What's his name?"

Maika told her and provided a birth date, as asked.

The officer entered the data base. "There is nothing on him in our records."

"Only because I didn't report it." Maika mentioned her Y2K incident.

"Ma'am, you raised him, you got him the way he is. We don't deal with domestic disputes", and hung up on Maika.

Maika phoned Eva. Only a voice mail answered. She left a message, demanding an explanation. In her trembling voice she asked for verification of the lease Ron claimed to sign with her.

Then Maika began to worry about Allan. What if Ron takes it out on him? Allan couldn't enter the house now and Ron might be right there to get in when Maika opens the door. This began to frighten her. She phoned a friend who lived in the immediate neighborhood. They've known each other for ten years and he might be able to bring Allan home. When he answered, he said that they had company and he was just leaving to rent a movie. He apologized and reminded Maika of the Y2K incident. He did not want to be involved with Ron.

Ron arrived with a friend, who drove him over. He obviously read the note on the front door and tried to get in through the back door, where another note was posted. He rang the doorbell and banged on the door, to no avail. Maika had her motion security alarm on – she stayed by the phone in her bedroom, where was one alarm terminal. She phoned the police again. Someone had written her name down and now the female officer was willing to talk to her. It was a different voice than the previous one and remained with Maika on the line till Ron left the premises. Then the officer gave her a case number and offered assistance on the phone, in case Ron would come back and threaten her. Maika found out later on that her neighbour friend drove by and when he saw Ron taking a computer into the van that parked on the driveway, he called the police that someone has broken into a garage of his friend during her absence. Based on his phone call, the police responded.

Ron and his friend drove away. Shortly after, the phone rang again. Maika was sure it was Ron. She would not pick it up. This time the message was much longer. In an angry voice Ron stressed his rights to enter the house and that Maika had no authority to change locks. This was going to be legally costly to her, he said. He reminded her again, that his sister was the only owner and she intended to sell the house for much less. He threatened his mother with legal action if any of his belongings are damaged or lost, and with a number of other conditions. At the end he wished her a Happy Mother's Day again. All the way through the phone call he sounded mean, but overly confident.

At this point, Maika phoned me and I replied "Is this real?" I would not come over and be with her. Ron frightened me. As much as I felt for my friend, and was concerned for Allan, I had no courage to face the situation. I know that Maika phoned another friend, who was in shock and promised to give her a call the following day. She advised Maika to write everything down, as it happened. Maika went downstairs to her computer and tried to clear her mind to write the affidavit. Each time she moved around the house, she had to disconnect the burglar alarm. It was not easy for Maika to write everything down as it happened. She worried about Allan and phoned the restaurant. He made himself available when told that it was urgent. Maika pleaded with him to leave work as soon as possible and to do it discretely through the kitchen back door and meet Maika in a nearby hotel. He was confused and unwilling to 'escape'. Maika told him quickly that something very unusual and serious happened and he must do as she says.

"Allan, I am not kidding. This is very serious! I had to change locks and you cannot get in without me. Stay away from Ron. I couldn't let you in if Ron is around. I'd rather pick you up and come with you home!"

Allan was very confused, but sensed that something unusual had happened between her and Ron.

"Allan, I will pick you up at midnight. Please, avoid Ron. I have a feeling that he is heading over there and will try to hurt me through you. Watch out for him. Please, be ready to be picked up at midnight. I will just drive by – be ready by the stairway. Call me when you are done with your shift!"

Maika continued writing the affidavit. Allan didn't call at all. Then Maika phoned Nick and asked him to come over, releasing just a part of information about the urgency. She was afraid that he would not come either. Nick did show up! He was in disbelief when Maika told him the story. He listened to Ron's messages recorded on the voice mail box.

"The guy is nuts!" he said. "This is a dirty blackmail! Does Jeff know?"

"I will call him in the morning. Now is too late and I need to write everything down. I cannot even think straight, never mind telling him what happened."

"Maika, as long as you have Jeff on the titles, no one can take your house away. I don't think Ron knows about him being involved and frankly, I think he is bluffing."

This was very comforting for Maika. For a moment she relaxed, but expressed a concern over Allan's safe return home. Nick offered to pick him up, but asked her to check first with the restaurant.

Maika phoned there right away. The hostess said that Allan was at the bar with his brother and then she went to get him. Allan sounded a bit drunk on the phone.

"Allan, get out of there so Ron doesn't notice. Go bathroom and then sneak out through the kitchen area. Please, do that soon. Nick will wait for you in the alley with his car." Maika made sure she was giving clear instructions.

"What are you talking about, Mom? Ron is my brother! We're just having a drink together and then I'll get home by cab." Allan didn't take Maika seriously.

"In that case, make sure Ron doesn't get into the same taxi, not even for a drop off. When will you be heading home?"

"Soon, Mom. Don't worry, alright!"

"Allan, don't say anything of what we've talked about to Ron. You must promise!"

While Maika spoke to Allan, Nick looked at her with great sadness. He couldn't resist a comment,

"Ron is having him brainwashed by now. Did all your children know how you acquired the house? I think you should've involved them more in your share of responsibilities. You seem to do everything by yourself! Has Allan offered to pay a part of your bills? He is working and making money now. If he lived elsewhere, he would have to pay rent!"

"I know, Nick, that I've been too soft with them. They have a long life full of responsibilities ahead of them. Allan is still young. He chose a trade instead of post secondary education. He saved me lots of hardships that way. I want him to enjoy himself a bit. He works long hours, as you know." Maika defended her way of mothering.

Nick listened again to the voice message from Ron. Then he listened to the first one. He suggested having them recorded and offered to do it. He felt that Ron's siblings should have a copy.

"He is a psychopath! His voice shifts, his words and the tone are full of anger, hatred, and also of desperation. He needed some money, didn't he?"

"The potential investors probably asked him for his financial contribution. Where else would he get it from than from this house sale?" Maika explained.

"Maika, it is also your fault. You shouldn't have taken him in. I warned you. He grew over your head. You always forgive and forget.

Kids need a strong hand. The parent isn't the authority anymore. Teachers lost it a long time ago and who else do young people respect and fear now?" Nick went quiet for a while, likely wondering what would be awaiting him one day.

Nick wasn't surprised when Maika told him how the police were trying to cop-out of involvement.

"Domestic disputes are unpredictable, and it is a private affair," he said. Then Nick reminded Maika to phone Allan's father and ask him to pick up his son.

"I already told him that possibly he'll have to take his son in for a few days, until the situation here is resolved. Ron would eventually use Allan to get into the house." Maika explained to Nick how Allan was slowly drifting away from his emotional co-dependence on his parents, wanting to grow up and individualize himself. On the contrary, his father couldn't accept that the boy was growing up and didn't want to speak with him daily, not returning his phone calls. Now he'll have a chance to enjoy his son. It will be good for both of them. Allan never lived with him. The weekend visits narrowed to Sunday visits and for the last year to an occasional meeting over coffee."

It was around three o'clock in the morning. Allan had not shown up, nor phoned. Nick was calming Maika down. She was beginning to imagine the worst. Just around that time, someone rang the doorbell. Maika was relieved to see Allan's face through the glass in the door. Before she unlocked the storm door for him, she checked if he was alone. He was. Relieved, she opened the door and asked where he was this long.

"I was with my brother!" he answered with a big smile on his face. He was a good drunk, friendly and cheerful.

"Ron cannot come here anymore, Allan. He did something very wrong and is involving other people into his scheme. Stay away from him! He is trouble!" Maika wanted to spare her son from the real story, to have him to enjoy life and to protect him from the darkness a while longer.

"I am taking you to your Dad's place. He is expecting you. Get some of your stuff packed. Take enough for one week. I can bring what you need later on."

"Why? Ron said I can stay here. It is my sister's house, Mom!"

"Is that what Ron told you? It is my house! I paid for it honestly! Eva hasn't contributed financially at all. Not a penny! True, she qualified me for the mortgage, but the house was always mine. She just posed legally as its owner. Ron has nothing to claim here!" Maika was upset again.

Nick interjected, "I will drive you to your Dad's place. Mom will stay here."

Allan went to his room to pack.

Nick talked Maika into calming down.

"You won't be able to stop Ron from brainwashing Allan. By now, he's done his number on him. They've been drinking for three hours! You could see it on Allan's face and you heard his words!" Nick observed Maika's tired face, her eyes full of desperation. "Call me tomorrow, Maika. I think you have nothing to worry about. Jeff is on the titles and without him they can do nothing. Finish your affidavit and try to get some sleep."

Both men left. It was about four o'clock when Maika received a call from Allan. He arrived at his Dad's. Maika tried to complete the affidavit. It was ready for Jeff to read. She had one hour to rest. Anxious to speak with Jeff, she phoned his home shortly after six. She knew that he was an early riser and walked his dog in the morning. He agreed to meet her in the park close to his residence.

Jeff came with his dog on leash. He read the affidavit and told Maika that Eva phoned him on Tuesday and asked him to come over to the lawyer's office on Friday to over sign the titles.

"What lawyer?" asked Maika.

"The same one who did the paperwork when the house was purchased. He is in the same office."

Maika was relieved that Eva has evaded her brother's scheme, by getting out of the game. In this case, Ron was just bluffing. Jeff suggested to Maika to see the lawyer on Monday. Jeff's daughter needed him to co-sign a large loan at this time. He wanted to be free of other financial involvements. He suggested to Maika to report Ron's threats against her person to the police. He reminded Maika of Y2K incident and was glad that she changed locks and protected Allan.

All this time the calm natured Jeff was nervous while dealing with Maika. She just thought that he was anxious to make a closure.

Eva could not be reached. Maika left a message for her, asking her to return a call. Then she completed the affidavit and tried to rest. She still didn't feel hungry. She drank more water than usual. The noon client came. He noticed Maika's tired features and that she wasn't herself. When he showed a sincere interest, Maika told him what happened. He responded, "How about that? The little bastards, they think they can get away with anything nowadays. Hang in there and don't give them any more of yourself!" He has been a schoolteacher for years.

Maika called another good friend. Talking was therapeutic and everyone understood her need. The friend was in shock. "Maika, I don't know what to say? How are you?"

"Broken up with the heart torn out of me. They casted lots for my garments!"

Linda was very compassionate. Being a mother herself, she could not imagine anything like that entering her life. She offered her time, ear, and money, if needed. Linda calmed Maika down, "On Monday you will feel better. You will sign the titles over to your name and move on. It will not be easy to forget this, never mind forgiving. In time, all will be healed."

"In my wildest dreams I would not imagine anything like this coming from my child. Ron has caused me so much pain and expenses in my life!"

"Tell me about it! If I didn't know you, I'd think you must've been a bad mother, having a son like him. The boy has criminal mind. He premeditated this!"

Maika had support she needed from her friends. Frank did not call that day. Police called. They wanted to know if she was alright. This pleased Maika very much. Then she drove over to the bank to make a payment with the post-dated cheque she had from a client. She dreaded the worst that the account did not exist anymore. First, she tried to insert the card into ATM machine to check the balance. The card was swallowed up and the monitor instruction suggested claiming it at the desk. This confirmed that Eva closed down the account. Allan was saying that Eva asked him for the card.

The next day, on the Mother's Day, Frank phoned in the late afternoon. He spoke of his wonderful children and how great time he had in the hill. They were celebrating Mother's Day now.

"Happy Mother's Day, Sweetie!" he wished Maika. "Have your children called you?" This was like a teasing question after all that has happened.

"Yes, as a matter of fact, I got earlier wishes on Friday and today Allan phoned just a few hours ago, right after he woke up. I'm having a memorable Mother's Day."

"I'm glad. How did you manage on Friday?" He could not evade the expected question.

"I did it my way." Maika wanted to be very brief. The moment she finished with the affidavit, she released all to the ethers and the higher justice.

"What happened?"

"A lot! I feel exhausted. Nick assisted me the way the friend would. I had pairs of ears that heard me out and tomorrow I am going to sign the titles over to my name."

"Oh, good! I was going to recommend it again," stated Frank. All the way, from the start of his phone call, he was impartial and detached, as if he spoke to the casual friend. Maika picked up on it right away.

"Do you have time to visit?" She chose to test her hunch.

"No, Sweetie. I don't think I could. We're having dinner here. They asked me to stay."

"I just thought I'd ask. Enjoy the evening, Frank." It was clear to Maika that her situation frightened Frank to the point that he decided to give his "ex" another chance.

Emotionally emptied, as she was, Frank's lack of empathy for her was bearable. She had another name to add to the list, less soul to mingle with, one more friend to part with and the lover to miss. In the void, anything is possible. If Maika's grail could be filled to the brim, it also could be emptied to its very bottom, and then … a new life wave enters the being and resurrection of the dead takes place. It was the Mother's Day she will never forget. The sorrowful mother she was – mater dolorosa.

THE COUP

THE lawyer asked Maika in, when he heard her name from the receptionist. He took out the file about the titles transaction and presented it to Maika to read.

"Where am I supposed to sign?" She was confused about the document.

The lawyer's face turned pale. He was almost as pale as she was, but she had reasons to be. After a short pause, he broke the moment of silence.

"Jeff signed it over here. He understood that you had temporary financial problems."

"The house was supposed to be signed over to my name! Not to remain on my daughter's name only! My house was taken away from me during my absence!"

The lawyer was anxious to know what preceded the misunderstanding on both sides. After Maika passed him the affidavit to read, she observed his inanimate face transforming him into a responsive and involved participant. When done, he looked at Maika with genuine sympathy.

"Your daughter told me that she was going to continue making mortgage payments for you until you recover financially!"

"She could have done that anyhow. She has never made any. This is more serious! Jeff was proxy for me, unaware of what was happening. The house is listed for sale. Ethically, Jeff had no right to get out of it without my consent. Legally, he could do it." Maika was crushed. Her trusted friend gave her house away. She could see that he owed her the equity. At this point, Maika could only count on Eva's conscience.

"What are we going to do?" she asked in desperation.

"Do you have all your documentation in place in regards to the house that would prove that you truly took on the owner's responsibility?"

"Well, I didn't hang onto every receipt about my mortgage deposits, but I could gather all of documentation in regards to renovations, insurance, utility payments and I paid for the down payment on the house with cheques. Plus, I have friends as witnesses who loaned me money for my down payment and I have cheques that they cashed. I have enough to work with!"

"Before you place the caveat against the title, let me speak to your daughter. I will phone her work place this afternoon and will let you know by tomorrow morning. I am so sorry that this happened to you! Such a nice lady … I cannot imagine you would hurt anyone… Your own children doing this to you! I really feel for you … "

In tears, Maika asked for advice. He suggested dealing with Jeff and asking him to talk to Eva as well. Then he told Maika that Eva came to his office on Thursday, paying for the transaction and rushed to have it signed off by Jeff latest Friday. Eva spoke of the listing and that she would forward the equity to her mother.

"That is hard to believe after all that has taken place, isn't it." Maika concluded.

"It takes almost a week time before the Titles Office does the transfer. If you place the request for caveat now, you are still several days behind. She is ahead of you."

As distraught as Maika was, she doubted that Eva would consent to the reversal of the titles. If she has gone thus far, she would keep on taking it further.

"So, I have to wait now and see. Well, the worst is behind me, now the legal action is ahead of me. What a Mother's Day gift I got!"

"I never heard of a case like this!" The lawyer's voice echoed with disbelief.

"Neither had I, but I am not a lawyer. You would have access to stories like this one, wouldn't you?"

"You'd imagine I would. Your daughter is a professional woman; she cannot afford doing this! I'll present her with consequences of her action. I am positive we'll have this resolved!"

Maika left his office with hope in her heart, but with a deeper disappointment about her daughter. Eva has teamed up with her brother after all. Ron was not bluffing when claiming that he signed the lease with his sister. Likely, Maika will never find out what blackmail Ron used on his sister, or what has turned them to be as dark in mind and heart to contemplate a betrayal like that on their mother. It was becoming too much for her strong and spirited nature; it was a heavy weight to carry on her small shoulders.

When Maika got home, she called Jeff immediately. She was brief, telling him that he signed her house away, likely not suspecting a foul play, but reminded him that under no circumstances he was to do that without her consent and never when she is out of town and cannot be reached.

"You gave my house to my daughter, Jeff. You owe me the equity. Are you ready to pay me?"

Jeff was speechless. Maika was not sure for a while that he remained on the other end of phone line.

"Jeff, you helped me to acquire the mortgage for this house. You were proxy for me on the titles. You were a key person and I had peace, because you were there for me. Now, it is gone. How will you solve this?"

"I guess I screwed up big time", he answered in a grave voice. "I will phone Eva. She lied to me. She said that you knew about this and that she was going to continue making payments on your behalf. The mortgage was at her name."

"And you needed to get out of it to help your daughter. It was a perfect timing, wasn't it?" Maika concluded.

"Yes, it was."

Nick happened to call the other line in this moment, thus liberating Jeff from further response. Maika explained Nick what happened. The unexpected news surprised him.

"I think you should take a direct legal action against Jeff. It will take too long with your kids. Not many lawyers will desire to represent your daughter, seeing the character she has. Jeff can take her to court, if he wishes. I thought he was a well-educated man! He's got his own company, hasn't he? Is he dumb, or what has clouded his mind?"

"Nick, I cannot take action against Jeff. He's been a good friend over the years. He tried to help me. His mind got clouded, just like mine. This whole affair has its origin elsewhere."

"Sure, your greedy son is behind it! You have short memory when it comes to bad experiences with people. What your kids have done is like a 'palace revolution', the 'coup'. The opposition takes over when the ruler is away. Now just focus on how to get your money out of it."

"It is more than money. It is a huge cross to bear. It looks like all three eldest children are a part of it and now Jeff. Now I know why Jeff was so nervous on Saturday when we met. He realized what he's done."

"What does Frank say about all this? He rushed you for the coast trip somewhat, didn't he?"

"Frank doesn't know much yet. He is in hiding in his cave of false securities."

"You didn't tell him?!" asked surprised Nick.

"He saw the house on Friday, but had to leave, having plans with his kids. He helped me to take Ron's heavy stuff out. He phoned on Sunday afternoon – just a superficial call. I didn't tell him much."

"Why? He should know! He is a part of it!"

"I think it scared him enough on Friday. Just the dream itself frightened him and how everything was falling into place. You know how Frank is! Everything has to be predictable. Imagine his children having had an encounter with mine, sometimes. That alone is a turn off. Besides, he is not the men's man."

"You should add him to the list. He is a part of the team!" suggested Nick.

"Ron said that he would break us up. He had him figured out, don't you think?"

"Look at the bright side: you handled it well so far, are intact and know who your friends are. You had far too many."

That made Maika smile. Nick always made her laugh. He was a gifted joke teller, creating in the moment of need to lighten up any situation. Maika looked for humorous side of life and tried to see the light at the end of a tunnel.

"There must be something very good behind all this, Nick. The lower we fall, the higher we fly, the worse something gets, the better things come out of it. I'll pull through this, but believe me; I wouldn't want to be in my children's shoes! There is heavy karma attached to what they've done."

Nick and Maika talked about their understanding of life events. Everything has its cause and that always creates effect. Six people, Maika included, have been directly involved in something that will have corresponding repercussions. It would only be a matter of time to see results.

THE SEQUEL

MAIKA didn't hear from the lawyer for two days. Though Jeff tried, he didn't succeed in reaching an agreement with Eva. She was determined to remain on the titles alone. Brad called. He wanted to know about her trip to the coast. Maika was releasing news slowly to him, talking about her grandson first.

"Any offers on the house?"

"I am taking it off the market, Brad. It is still listed, but no offer will be accepted for some time."

"What made you change your mind, Maika? Are you reconsidering my proposal?" asked hopeful Brad.

Maika began to unveil the news. There were moments when Brad interjected with "I am so sorry to hear that" or "this is unbelievable".

"Are you alright, Maika? How are you coping?" asked concerned Brad.

"Without a support from friends I would not be coping at all. I cannot sleep, am exhausted, totally unfit to take any client."

"Now I understand my mission!" exclaimed Brad. "I was to prevent this! You didn't have to go through this if you accepted my offer. Didn't we talk about sealing the deal for the first of May?"

"Brad, how many times did I remind myself of this fact!? It is amazing how Universe is offering us choices, protecting us or releasing us into the next lesson of our lives, almost testing our readiness."

"What a lesson! I think I made a right choice by not having children. If you knew what was awaiting you in life, would you have those kids?"

"I am sure I will be asked this question more times. Unfortunately, I have to say that regardless of what has transpired, I would have chosen to have children. They bring into our lives the greatest lessons and challenges. We are free to part from friends, allow them to come into our lives and leave when the relationship matures and fulfills its purpose, but with children and other direct family members we are stuck for life. The selection of various levels of human encounters is organized at another level of consciousness, I am sure."

"Do you think that I am depriving myself of experiencing life fully by being single and childless?" Brad was serious with his question.

"If you had family, Brad, you would not be able to work as many hours as you are now. Your job orientation and performance is good for all life. Perhaps, the family life is outside the scope of your required experiences for this lifetime. The all-knowing Soul is directing your steps in life. Enjoy what you have and live it fully."

"I could have saved you from the situation you're having now. My Soul guided me in that direction," concluded Brad, with an evident sorrow in his voice.

"Yes, you could have, but I didn't allow it. I chose this, instead. I must have been ready for it, don't you think? Maybe I wrote the script myself."

"You should be a soap opera writer, Maika! I am anxious to hear about the next sequel!"

Maika laughed. She appreciated any kind of uplifting mood at this time.

Brad recognized Maika's good spirit, despite the hardship she was enduring now. He promised he'd call her again soon. He kept his promise and called almost daily with a question "How is the soap opera sequel developing?" Maika updated him each time. Doubtlessly, Brad was an important character in her story.

Frank showed up. He had a half an hour, he said. Maika asked him to take her to the post office to pick up an Xpresspost she received a notice for. It was delivered on Monday when she wasn't home. Frank was concerned and was not surprised that the letter was from Eva. Eva sent her mother a Notice of Eviction with the tenancy termination date due in two weeks. The reason was the 'illegal act against the landlord' by changing the locks without permission of property owner/landlord. Eva wrote information on the envelope in her own handwriting. Frank was surprised that Maika took it well, as if she expected the news. She was not ready to convey to him what happened over the weekend at this point of time.

The lawyer invited Maika to his office on Thursday morning. He provided her with copies of documents she'd need for placing a lien and offered to provide information her new hired lawyer would need. He rushed Maika to act fast, as the long weekend was approaching and would slow down the action. He regretted to fail in dealing with Eva, who refused to add her mother to the titles. He explained to Eva that her mother was forced to take the matter to the law and that Eva had no chance of having any judge's sympathy nor getting a decent representation. "There may be one lawyer in our association who would take her as a client," he said to Maika, "you will need that in order to get ahead with this case." He acknowledged that Eva was harsh and determined to pursue in her intention, whatever it was. Maika was concerned about the mortgage payments being made, but at this point had no way of finding out. The lawyer assured her that Eva would not sabotage her credit and would not go as far. Maika had a cash in hand to cover for three payments, asking the lawyer to keep it in trust, but he suggested asking the new lawyer for that. He was shocked hearing about the eviction notice.

On her return home, Maika phoned a friend who was familiar with law firms in town. She phoned one and they referred her to an established firm that specialized in family matters. Maika booked the earliest appointment available for Friday afternoon. Jeff agreed to come along and pay for the services. He was remorseful about his action and desired to correct it.

Frank showed up on Friday. He apologized for his lack of involvement, admitting to his fear. Maika was just editing her affidavit when he came. Frank was reading over her shoulder.

"Aren't you embellishing a bit?" he asked.

"It is written the way it happened, Frank." Maika was numb in emotions by now.

"Sweetie, why didn't you tell me about it?"

"I needed strong and sincere people around me, Frank. I needed the problem solvers, not the worriers. You can help by driving me and Jeff to the appointment. We have to pick him up first. I hope you have time to do that." Maika's voice was impartial.

"Of course, anything …" was Frank's answer. Maika could feel the residue of cowardice still emanating from him. No matter what he would do or say, the memory could not be erased. Frank was not available during the most difficult moments of her life. He gathered enough courage, though, to question Jeff about his own failure. Jeff was slightly evasive with answers, but committed to help Maika in solving the case.

The hired lawyer also questioned Jeff regarding his participation in transaction.

"What is your profession, Sir?"

When Jeff answered, the lawyer looked straight into Maika's face and suggested to take a shortcut and deal with Jeff only.

"If I deal with your daughter and am to succeed, she still must accept and sign up for my mail delivery and, if she has no representation, it will be a lengthy process, costly to you."

Jeff assured him that he'd pay for the fees. He wrote a cheque for three thousand dollars to cover for the initial legal fees and the caveat. Once cashed after the long weekend, the firm would place a caveat against the titles of Maika's home and block Eva from a possible private sale of the property. Jeff was asked to find out from the bank if any mortgage payment was made during a month of May. His name was still attached to the loan at this time and Maika could catch up with payments to avoid foreclosure on the property.

The entire matter had to rest over the weekend – the longest weekend Maika could remember. She just had to remind herself that the worrier now is the hired lawyer and that she must focus on her health and income.

Linda came over to visit. She fully empathized with Maika and offered a loan to spare Maika from more stress. "What the friends are for?" she always responded. Linda's been in Maika's life for over ten years now. Both of European roots, they had more in common than average. They also shared their spirituality; both have given up on religious organizations as a way to enlightenment. Frank was a church going Christian. Lucy and her husband were attending Sunday services of their Christian protestant faith. Nick was a self-made spiritual seeker, inclined to Zen Buddhism as a tool for life. Maika was a practitioner, accepting gifts in all kinds of wrappers that life prepared for her. She knew that God loved her!

Another lady friend of many years phoned and asked about the house sale and Maika's plans for the future. When Maika briefly informed her about the news, the friend felt offended that Maika hasn't phoned in time of need.

"I didn't think you needed a burden like that. You chose a childless life. I am reaping consequences of my choice," explained Maika.

Her friend was a thinker, a seeker of her truth. She quickly came up with a question: "Have you done anything lately that dealt with martyrdom?"

"Interesting that you ask," Maika responded. "Yes, as a matter of fact, I went with Frank to walk the Way of the Cross at Easter time."

"Why did you do that?" The friend was upset.

"I did it for Frank. He wasn't clear on the meanings of stations, so I explained each mystery as it reflects in our lives. When I got to the "stripping of the garments", I paused for a while. I questioned my own life. I thought that this mystery was done to me in my previous marriage! I guess it was just an introduction to it."

"You attracted this," the friend said.

"Possibly … I thought it should rest with my past… I was not as eager to do the walk with Frank at first. You know that I put feelings into everything and they trigger reaction, but then I thought it would bring us closer," concluded Maika.

"Frank is not of your level, Maika! More you grow into your future-self, more he is going to fall behind. Sure, you can help him through his journey, but … shouldn't he be allowed getting there at his own pace? He is of your past!"

"I've known that for some time. When you love the person, you make all kinds of sacrifices. You've done that too!"

Both women talked about relationships with the beloved people, about the difference each intimate encounter creates in our life, about its ups and downs and the energy dynamics that are beyond our control. No matter how many wonderful lovers we have had in our lives, the most intimate and permanent relationship is with our own Soul, the representation of God.

SEQUEL ONE

THE caveat document was signed and delivered to the Land Titles Office in the mid of the following week. A courier service was hired to deliver a letter to Eva, informing her about the possible pending legal action against her. She was offered a compromise. The courier could not reach Eva at her residence, neither at her place of work for three weeks. She intentionally prolonged the action. Then she hired a lawyer who kept on corresponding with Maika's lawyer without a resolve and progress. Jeff found out that four mortgage payments were not made. Clearly, Ron did not pay a rent to Eva and she did not assume responsibility of the property owner. Linda's loan assisted Maika to catch up with immediate expenses. The payments were made personally in a bank on Jeff's behalf. Eva's negligence was the only advantage Maika had over her daughter at this time, who shortly after made a couple of payments, rushed to have the house insurance and property tax monthly payments transferred for withdrawals from her own account, thus creating another obstacle to Maika's attempt to maintain her status. She became a caveator for sixty days instead.

Frank kept on reminding Maika to let Allan and Lucy know what has been happening. Maika wanted to spare Lucy, but agreed to inform Allan. When he read the affidavit, he had difficulty believing the content at first, but finished reading it regardless. There was silence, a long pause before him or Maika said anything. He was sad.

"Now you understand why you had to stay with your father, Allan. As soon as matters are settled, you can move back here."

Allan admitted that the long commute on the public transit to his father's place was tiring, though on many late nights his father picked him up. Maika never discussed her older children's conduct with Allan. She chose to leave it to his judgment. After all, they were his only siblings and if only one of them remained a loyal friend to him for life, he would not be alone when his both parents are gone. It was about preserving the surviving family ties, the bond of one generation.

Maika began to accept appointments again and to focus on her work. Allan moved back and cheered his mom up with his smile and sense of humour. She kept on picking him up after his late shifts. Maika's friends kept in touch, often dropped by for a chat, or to offer a word of comfort. All of them condemned Eva and Ron for what they've done, but mostly spared Maika from thoughts of the recent past. When we asked if it was the money from the house sale they wanted, or was it something else, Maika told us that she offered a reward sum of five thousand to Eva. "You helped me to be able to buy this place, you can use the money to reduce your student loan," she told her daughter. Eva resolutely refused and repeated that it is her mom's money and she herself doesn't need more. Maika gave her enough household items over the years, helped with cat sitting when Eva was on holidays, just as she promised. The relationship between the two of them was good. Eva had noble interests she shared with her mother and often they spoke about their private matters. Just around the time of listing Eva told Maika how fortunate mother she was, having four children who are smart, healthy, are multi-talented, self-motivated and are addiction free, except Ron, who smokes. Maika responded to that comment with gratitude. She truly had three great children of the four! How could a human being change so suddenly? Are there unseen forces influencing human behaviour? Ron and Eva acted in synchronicity in time and space, as if they made an agreement. Maika's dream prepared her ahead of time to be ready for the betrayal. She truly was screwed three times behind her back! Why is this happening to Maika, who's been so committed to her role of a mother, to her work, clients and friends? We had a number of discussions on the subject of trials and tribulations and that we are responsible for what is happening in our lives.

"Do you think it has anything to do with your past lives actions?" we asked.

Maika didn't oppose our question, but commented on other explanations, such as 'what we have or have not done in this lifetime', our choices we have made. She kept on reminding us that she doesn't regret her choices and has followed her heart all the way. If she followed the reason only, she'd accept Brad's offer. Her teachers were sages of all times and she often reminded us of the words of Lao-tzu: 'What is the good man, but the bad man's teacher? What is the bad man, but the good man's job? If you don't understand this, you will get lost, no matter how intelligent you are. It is the great secret.'

"The dilemma of a parent lies in emotions. It touches us deeply when our child does wrong or something happens to it", Maika expanded on her reflection. "There is an ethereal umbilical cord the mother has to her child. The emotional energy leaks into the ethers, or is absorbed by the subject that caused the upset and pain. Any co-dependent relationship is unhealthy. Parent's challenge is to detach when children are adults and let them live in their own reality on their own stage of life. I have likely completed my affairs with my older children. Every thought and emotion creates a strong imprint on the screen of matrix of consciousness. Maybe mine were interfering with their lives and the way they wanted to live it."

As sad as Maika was about her realization, we wondered why her detachment had to happen in such a drastic way. What is it about Maika that she is forced into separation from some of her adult children? The amazing synchronicity with so many other 'rescue operations' presented to Maika's awareness indicated that there was an intervention coming from other levels of consciousness that successfully involved Ron, Eva, Brad, Frank, Jeff and perhaps even Lucy.

"Eva's assistance in the mortgage qualification was a good deed, but she totally annulled it with her action now" lamented Maika. "Eventually, I will understand what brought her to this. Surely, Ron had an influence on her, but she had more than a month now to correct what has been done. It is entirely in her hands now. She is drafting her own future, not mine." Maika was beginning to see the event from the point of an observer.

We, mature parents, could not disagree with Maika's reflection. We felt that Eva was on a dangerous 'Power Trip' and we wondered if she and Ron would be forgiven in time. The healing takes time.

SEQUEL TWO

THE property listing expired. Maika began to sort her household for a yard sale. She was willing to part with her living room furniture, her beautiful mature house plants, many household items and some artwork. Proceeds paid her utility bills. She preserved some good furniture for Allan's imminent apartment in downtown. The less she was to own, the freer she was to be. Maika planned to spend some time with her mother who lived in Europe and also hoped to revisit with friends and relatives. With a smile she told us that she'd like to be a 'no mad nomad' for a while, to contemplate her life and prepare for her future. We knew that she'll make it. She had skills none of us possessed; she was able to survive under many conditions in many environments. Where ever the life wave would direct her, she was willing to adapt and accept. "As long as I have a garden around me, I will be content", she repeated to us. Many of us thought that she'd move to Vancouver to be closer to her grandson and Lucy, but Maika specified that this time she has to open up to her life's calling. "I will be given directions, don't worry", she always said. By now, we acknowledged that an exceptionally reliable guidance was coming through her dreams. This fascinated us! Some of us took workshops to learn how to meditate, we practiced yoga or some other form of spiritual exercise, listened to all kinds of 'teachers and speakers', read books about spirituality and lives of saints, but none of us could compare our lives with hers. She just kept on living her days and enjoyed the ride with all its twists and turns. This sometimes frightened Frank. He could not point his finger at the real source. And just like all of us, he waited for the next sequel of her life. Maika was the only one who could turn the page and resume her story. No other novel, or fiction, could be as satisfying as hers. There was always something new happening and we were allowed to participate on the real stage and be given a chance to do our part. She said it herself, that whatever we've done as a team, was ordained and keeps us as a team for eternity. That was very exciting! The eternity concept is gratifying; it gives us an identity of a divine being trapped in a physical body passing through existence in time and space. A team or group work must be having a greater impact than an attempt of a single individual.

Maika missed her grandson and longed to see him, but we advised her to wait till the house situation progresses and she is clear. The lawyers didn't reach any agreement yet to give Maika some level of certainty and relief. She phoned Lucy and mentioned her intention to visit around the third week of July. Lucy said that they will be away camping at that time. Maika was pleased to hear about the normalcy Lucy was incorporating into her life now and responded with fervor, "Where?"

"None of your business," was Lucy's quick reaction.

Maika could hardly believe her daughter's answer, defending her own curiosity,

"I just wanted to know about your holidays! I have no slightest intention of going with you! I only want to see you, guys and leave again. Babies are growing so fast..."

"You know, Mom, when you were here last time, you weren't much of help. Unless you do things the way I do, it is not helping at all." Lucy's tone of voice was condescending and malicious.

Maika was in shock. Is this her daughter, now a mother speaking? Yes, it was Lucy. Maika revisited with memories that she hoped to forget. Almost everything she did for Lucy's family in May was criticized. The cookies from Lucy's recipe box were either too brown, or unfinished. The stew had to be made with the exact brands of sauces and additives named on the recipe card. Maika's home cooking wasn't good enough in her daughter's house – she had to do as expected. When changing a diaper, she either did it too soon after the previous change, or not frequently enough. When bottle feeding the baby, she held him too upright. When Maika intended to initiate a conversation on common subjects, she was cut off by words "It is only an assumption, mother!" It was a form of tyranny! Now Maika could not forget anymore, though she wanted to.

"Well, if you feel that way … I would not be helping this time; I would just pay a short visit and see my grandson for a while," she said with resignation.

Lucy assured her that she'd discuss a visit with her husband first.

Maika called me right away. She was crying and weeping like a child, her words were chopped while she was trying to describe what was said.

"Breathe deeply, Maika. Calm down. Take your time…."

After hearing Maika's testimony, I was shocked too. Without any doubt, Lucy was a part of the betrayal team. Three thrusts from behind her back represented her three children. Maika never told me earlier about the way Lucy treated her. She thought that it was due to hormonal changes that cause an uncontrollable pattern of behaviour women suffer with sometimes after having babies. Maika has observed for some time the rapid shifts in the tone of her daughter's voice. Depending to whom she was speaking, everyone received a special treatment, and that included her husband, neighbours, her in-laws, strangers and now her mother. The intonation and nature of the voice seemed familiar – it was a discernible auditory signature her three eldest children had in common.

Fortunately, Linda came to visit with Maika that same afternoon. She brought a sage to plant in Maika's herb garden and I decided to give her one of my lavender plants. The garden could use a new member and brighten its faithful custodian.

Nick called and offered an ear. He insisted that under no circumstances Maika should travel and leave the city.

"Everything is still fresh, Maika! Lawyers haven't resolved anything. You just have to see your grandson later," he stressed.

"I would be away for three days, maybe four!"

"Hello!" Nick accentuated the word, "The adversaries are just waiting for another trip of yours! I bid Lucy will change her mind and invite you. Don't let a sentiment to take over your reason. Forget about any trip for a while!"

Maika respected Nick's counsel and decided to postpone the trip.

"You know what you should do? Hire a lawyer to watch over your hired lawyer. The guy is cunning. You are doing all the groundwork while he is writing ineffective 'love' letters to Eva's lawyer."

"I am trying to save some money on fees, Nick."

"Not in their books! I bid they're laughing how much they'll make on the case!"

Nick was right on. Lucy called back the next day. Maika could visit after all. Apparently, the campgrounds have been booked for months and nothing was available. She was invited for a short visit before the long midsummer weekend. It was a very tempting proposition to which Maika answered with apprehension. She recalled Nick's advice.

"I have to think about it, Lucy. It is not the best timing for me. I'll let you know when I could come," she answered bluntly and thanked Lucy for her reconsideration.

Maika phoned Nick right after the call. He asked her to check the caveat related documents. Indeed, the caveat was expiring right before the long weekend.

"Another coincidence?" suggested Nick. "From now on you should be suspicious of anyone of the parties involved. It is a good exercise for you – it deals with harsh reality of the earthly existence. This grounds you more than anything else. Be vigilant! Ron is a con-artist, Eva is an ego driven personality and Lucy is facing her own darkness. It has nothing to do with their upbringing. They are adults fully responsible for their action. You are responsible for yours. So, don't goof!"

Nick was a gem. He was direct and sincere. Each time Maika phoned him, she was sure to hear "What's up?" It had an essence of lightness and stewardship.

What are the friends for? They're the greatest treasure in our lives participating in dynamics of our personalities and our true nature. They identify our strength and weakness. They are mirrors and reflectors of our issues and the many garments that veil our innocent nakedness. They are gifts from God.

THE CUCKOO NEST

THERE was no need to call any lawyer. He reminded himself by asking for additional five thousand dollars to cover for his fees. Jeff was ready to pay for it, but Maika offered to represent herself, "I can do it on my own, Jeff. Eva has a lawyer now and he has to deal with me. No more love letters! I will personally deliver my proposal to him and offer Eva a fair deal."

"Are you sure you want to do it, Maika? You know that I am willing to help out!"

"I know that, Jeff and I do appreciate. Let me give it a try first."

Maika called the lawyer about her decision. He was not happy about it and told her that possibly the matter has to go to court when caveat is expiring, but after speaking with her further, he offered his assistance if she needed it. He sent a letter to Eva's lawyer about Maika's choice.

Maika went to see Eva's lawyer. He was young and ambitious. He told Maika that her daughter was anxious to resolve the matter as fast as possible and was offering Maika to get her own mortgage on the house in order to clear her. Jeff made an appointment with a mortgage broker in his bank. He had two properties with clear title, and his company. Though he co-signed for his daughter's loan, he had enough assets to back up the mortgage. It wasn't enough for the bank. The house had only twenty percent equity.

About this time of July, Allan had his birthday. He told his mom that Ron will pick him up and treat him to a dinner. The brothers were to celebrate. Maika was just raking the mowed grass in the front yard when Ron drove fast into the cul-de-sac and stopped right in front of her house. While running the engine of his car, he had a loud conversation with someone on a cell phone. His arrogant entry bothered Maika and she decided to speak with him regarding the garage. Ron has not moved his car and many boxes from there yet. The door was still disabled. As she was approaching him with the question, he told her that she was not to speak to him and asked if his lawyer called her yet.

"Your imaginary lawyer didn't call me and you should be more careful with what you're saying in front of your imaginary friend that you are speaking with on your cell right now" and she walked back to her chore.

Shortly after Allan left with Ron. Maika was calm. She had capacity to treat herself with carefree moments. She was in her garden.

Other friends called Maika, inviting her for lunch. They saw her last after she listed her house and they asked her opinion on the market value of their home. They lived close by. Maika suggested a price that surprised and gladdened them. If their house sold for the price, they could fulfill their dream of many years to move to south-central British Columbia and acquire a property they had their eyes set on for some time. This time they phoned to tell her that they followed her advice and hired a consensual realtor. The house sold in two hours after the listing for the full asking price! Maika was very happy for them. They were willing to move out in three weeks. Maika met them many years ago through a Catholic Church. On occasion, they ran into each other, but being busy with their own families, they remained an acquaintance and now were reaching out to each other again. Walking by Maika's house, they noticed that For Sale sign was taken off. They assumed that the house was sold. Then Maika revealed her story to them. Astounded, they expressed a deep sympathy.

"I wouldn't speak to my children ever again if they've done anything like it", said Keith. His wife agreed. Jenny neither could forgive anything like it.

Then Keith paused for a while and stated, "This is like a story of cuckoo nest! The cuckoo bird lays her eggs in other smaller bird nest and the little bird sits on them, then feeds the hungry chicks that grow bigger and bigger and when they are big enough to overthrow their caring parent from the nest, they take over. It keeps on happening over and over again."

"Until one little bird sees through it and stops feeding, which will never happen in bird's life," concluded Maika.

"Are you taking care of it legally?" asked Keith.

Maika told them about the process and her intent. They were supportive and empathetic.

"When you sell, come to visit us. We already paid a down payment on our dream property. Our offer was accepted. It is beautiful there! It is an environment you would appreciate. We can create a high self-sufficiency. Maybe something will be available for you around there. Your equity would get you something and likely you would be able to make a small mortgage payment. You can work from home there too, as you know!"

It has been heart-warming to experience the outpouring compassion from friends. In gratitude, Maika decided to have a 'potluck garden party'. She hasn't sold her patio furniture yet and her emptier living room would provide a marvelous dance floor. Everyone offered to contribute and promised to show up. Unfortunately, Keith and Jenny could not make it, living far away. Even a contractor who applied an epoxy stone treatment on Maika's front door steps was invited. There was a change in Maika's household. Her ex-boyfriend found her a nice roommate who was happy to find a good and inexpensive place.

The party was success. Frank came and friends of many years showed up, including some from dance classes. Brad regretted that he was not available on that day and made up by taking Maika to Grass and Blues Festival later on, where they danced together.

At this time, Maika was waiting to hear about Eva's response to the proposal she presented to her lawyer. It was protecting Maika and was fair to Eva. To everyone's surprise, it was declined. The requested conditions were reasonable. Was this a way to force Maika into hiring a lawyer?

Maika e-mailed me the proposal draft. It was intended to protect Eva's interest and to accommodate Maika's; all points and conditions were clearly described in seven paragraphs. It was a balanced document. If signed, both parties would gain what they hoped to accomplish. To everyone's disappointment, it wasn't accepted. Eva wanted more; she wanted a total power over her mother's fate. Her refusal was controversial. She had her lawyer believing that the only concern was the mortgage liability she had with the house. She would agree to sell the house "By owner", but was not willing to recognize her mother as the owner, yet was claiming that she'd forward all assets from the sale to her. Maika emphasized the fact that property would not be sold to anyone who would need to assume the existing mortgage. The title would be clear. It was becoming a vicious circle, with no way to end the dispute. Maika was becoming exhausted and needed a break from it all. Then Eva's lawyer phoned and suggested to Maika to go ahead with the sale 'By owner" and not to be concerned about receiving the equity.

"Your daughter will pay it out to you. I know that for sure. She said it many times. I am giving you my word that she will. She just wants to reach an end to this and move on." He was trying to persuade Maika that her daughter could be trusted.

"Mr. Klein, she refused to sign the proposal that included all these points. How can I believe that she had a change of heart?"

"I think she was reactive at first and refused to sign it, but she is changing her mind now. She just wants to receive one thousand dollars toward my fees and get her piano that she has in your home," replied the lawyer.

"Mr. Klein, how can I believe that she won't change her mind again? Will I receive any confirmation from her in writing?" Maika could not afford another mistake.

"She likely won't, but you have my word on this."

"Your word ... No witnesses ... no written document."

At this point, Maika didn't know if Mr. Klein was trying to help and get the case over with, or was he insidious, testing her vulnerability. She couldn't surrender to trust.

"Mr. Klein, are you asking me to trust my daughter, or you?" asked cautious Maika.

"You can trust me! I am giving you my word!" He sounded persuasive and quite sincere.

"But you are a lawyer! You go by written word! I know that I cannot trust my daughter. What makes you believe that you could trust her?"

The lawyer seemed frustrated, getting nowhere with Maika. He likely hoped to instigate a closure, or force Maika into hiring a lawyer again. They usually make agreements and discuss the protocol with each other.

"Do you agree to pay your daughter the one thousand she is asking for and give her the piano?"

"She'll get the piano when the house is sold. I gave it to her six years ago and paid for each and every move of it. I became its caretaker. About the money? I find it unethical and immoral. She's got nerves!" responded Maika.

"Based on the approval of these two conditions, you will be given six weeks to sell the property "By owner" at your chosen price and would receive proceeds of the sale. After that your daughter will list it herself for a lower price, I'm sure."

"Unless I am on the titles, I am not feeling comfortable without a written agreement. I'm sorry and may be sorry later on, but this is the way I feel, Mr. Klein." Maika was sad and emotionally drained. Maybe she missed on the opportunity. She continued making mortgage payments and was always on time with her other expenses. Her clients relaxed after the house was taken off the market and kept on booking their appointments. Frequently they asked about Maika's future plans and where she would be practicing from, but at this point of time, she had no idea herself.

Frank showed up once in few days. It was becoming obvious that the relationship was weak and nearing its closure. He pretended being involved by asking questions regarding negotiations, but Maika perceived that his concern was principally revolving around assets and 'what if' she loses and just increases her debts.

It was on one of those short visits, while Frank and Maika enjoyed a beverage on a sunny patio when a doorbell rang. Maika rushed through the yard to see who was at her front door. It was Mr. Klein, Eva's lawyer. He personally served a letter to Maika along with a Notice of Termination of Tenancy effective in fourteen days.

"I don't think it's going to happen!" contested Maika.

"Are you going to get a lawyer now?" were the last words of Mr. Klein.

Maika showed the Notice to Frank. They read together the reasons for termination of tenancy: Non-Payment of rent; Changing of locks without consent of the Landlord; Renovation of premises without consent of the Landlord.

"What are you going to do now?" asked startled Frank.

At first, Maika trembled, but composed herself readily, endorsing her own status,

"First of all, I am not a tenant. The house is mine and I am making mortgage payments. I have passed Mr. Klein a cheque for all those payments Eva is making on my behalf and for the property tax. I will check my bank statement if it was cashed. I'll keep on doing it as long as I live here."

Frank had an absent gaze in his eyes. Maika was familiar with his pattern by now; it was discernible that she won't see him for some time. After he left, Maika phoned her former lawyer and asked for advice. He suggested another caveat, but felt that the case should go to court. This was going to be costly. Maika called Linda right after. Linda confirmed that Eva was a conniving person and that Maika should hire a lawyer.

"I already talked to him, Linda. He'll take it on."

"Do you have money to pay him?" asked concerned Linda.

"No, but Jeff will pitch in," assured her Maika.

"Let me pay for your lawyer."

"Why should you?"

"I have selfish reasons too. I don't want to hear another line about your incompetent lawyer and the hardship caused to you. I will pay for the lawyer of my choice, never the other one. He hasn't done much while he could. I know an honest lawyer. He's got a back bone. I've known him since he was a boy. He carries on with the Law firm his father owned, also a lawyer."

Maika was speechless for a while. She was in tears and humbly replied to Linda,

"I can pay you back from the house equity, not before."

"You don't need to pay me back anything. My children shared an inheritance with me they received from a distant relative. This lawyer will not overcharge. Can I call him for an appointment?"

"Yes, Linda. Yes, please!"

THE SOLACE

LIFE shifts embrace more than a challenge and testing ground; they involve every aspect of the individual going through transformation and they touch every person and individual consciousness sharing the process, whether voluntarily or not. The key player is the attractor of events and participants. The key instigator of the shift completes with the task and resumes with his/her own affairs and often departs from the scene. Not a one player is unqualified for the homework and task. Consciousness is kind, compassionate, loving, wise, all-knowing and all-present. Universe has every omni you can imagine on the scale of total goodness. One person's virtue may be a vice for another person. It is all relative, depending on the level of the observer and the observed. There is balance in everything. The quantum mechanics works in synergy with totality and wholeness, and always in harmony with the highest goal. Human race is passing through a gate from which there is no return. An accomplishment that is earnestly attained cannot be cancelled. Universe doesn't write cancelled cheques, neither there is a non-sufficient fund on the account. It is a trust fund. It gives you a credit, but is not a long term creditor. We are expected to pay back. Universal mind, or consciousness, is an inexhaustible storehouse of information and data, of solutions, ideas, resources and love. It is perfect. It won't judge; it will understand. It will teach and evolve all life. It is the causality of everything. In its projected world of effect, the history takes place.

A seeming chaos is the perfect order functioning within the most efficient economical structure imaginable. It gives importance to every coincidence and synchronicity; there is no waste. It is magical to the observed. To the observer it is awesome!

Linda kept her word and arranged one hour appointment with her highly endorsed lawyer. He heard Maika out, collected the required documentation and assured her that he'll have fast results. That same afternoon he phoned Eva's lawyer and an agreement was in making. Lucy didn't want Maika to visit them anymore. There was an evident misunderstanding on Lucy's part, something so distant and estranged that Maika proscribed to delve on at this time. Frank was out of picture for some time now.

A dear friend, almost a brother figure in Maika's life phoned her and enthusiastically spoke of someone he met with in Ireland, amongst other Canadian engineers. He spoke of him with reverence and felt the two of them should know about each other. He asked Maika to contact him by e-mail. The initial letter she sent him was brief and neutral. The immediate response to it was intriguing and fascinating. Marc was just writing his journal, asking to meet someone of his level. He regarded Maika's e-mail as the answer to his request. They kept in correspondence for three weeks, till the day of his arrival. All of us friends who knew about this upcoming visit were cheering for Maika. Linda gave her a gift of three hundred dollars, another friend brought a popular Australian red wine for Marc and her, and I know there was more offered and gratefully accepted. Maika could enjoy all five days of the visit. We just were anxiously waiting to hear from her. Marc was a mysterious stranger to us all.

Allan was already moved out to his own apartment downtown, which spared Maika from the late night driving in this upcoming winter season and, Maika had an additional bedroom available for visitors.

I've met with Maika right after Marc's departure. She phoned me during his visit, providing me with sufficient material that made me very impatient and eager to hear more. I thought they hit the roof and lost the ground. She spoke of metamorphosis and other phenomenal manifestations. I rushed over to Maika's with my laptop and allowed her plenty of time to describe what happened.

"When I was waiting for Marc at the airport, I was calm. I had a photograph of him, he had mine. I pretty well knew whom to expect. To my surprise, I was approached by an older man, slightly taller than me, holding a bouquet of flowers. He looked different to me than Marc from the picture, though his features were there. He asked me, 'Is that you?' and I said 'Yes, it's me. Marc?' He nodded. Flowers were beautiful; lots of lilies. We walked toward the parking lot, saying hardly anything, outside the common 'How was your flight?'."

"Did you like him? What was the first impression?" I asked.

"Bonnie, after so many disappointments in the past year, I was fully accepting the way it was. Okay, he looked older than he claimed to be, and he was maybe five foot seven. He followed me between parked cars. I opened the passenger side door for him first and turned around to walk toward my side. Marc was in my way, but he looked tall now, at the least six foot two inches. He embraced me around the waist, pressed himself against me and gave me a kiss that made my head spin. The energy emanating from his heart was incredibly loving and penetrating. He took my breath away! I was seeing a younger and taller man in Marc's body!"

"Malka" I had to ask, "were you eating enough that day and were you hydrated?"

"I know why you are asking me, Bonnie. When we both sat in a car, I checked him out often, just to make sure I was not hallucinating. He remained in that appearance for the entire visit. He just looked different at the airport!"

This introduction was so fascinating, that I asked Maika to narrate the story on a cassette tape twice. I couldn't afford to miss anything.

Marc had an unusual abundance of psychic energy. He claimed to be able to consciously connect to other manifestations of consciousness of the past, present and future. He was almost a channel, but fully present. He was not a medium. He never took drugs, neither in earlier years. He didn't even drink a coffee. He was dedicated to his diet, eating clean foods, as he put it. For a long time, he has been interested in a higher learning and was seeking out people who had acquired a respectable level of understanding the Universe. He was equally interested in science and especially in technology that would improve our environment. He said that he was working for "The Mother". Under no circumstances he was a 'new age junkie'. Knowing Maika well, she would not fall for the false or fake in this area.

At first, Marc dealt with jet lag, sleeping daytime more than nighttime. That gave Maika time to be with her clients. She and Marc spent enough time together to get to know each other and share their thoughts. Marc, without knowing what recently transpired in Maika's life, insisted that she went through a very unusual year, marking her new era.

"You served your family and now your family is liberating you from that responsibility. A new level of service is ahead of you, Maika."

Was he as perceptive? She wondered. Then he asked what exactly happened, Maika gladly volunteered to tell him, since he was seeing the world from other levels of observation and understanding.

His first words were,

"You are so lucky to pass the initiation and maintaining who you are!"

"What initiation?" asked puzzled Maika.

"Of the Crucifixion, gal!" was his joyous energetically charged answer.

Maika retreated into her thoughts. This time the Simon didn't help to carry her cross, Women of Jerusalem wept, there was the obvious Stripping of her garments and the intent of gaining from it, and the most painful moment of her life, when those whom she loved the most, had crucified her. There were witnesses watching in disbelief, unable to prevent this.

"Congratulations! You passed what many of us fear, knowing subconsciously that it is in our future, somewhere, sometime."

"What's next?" asked Maika solemnly.

"Good news! New Life! New relationships, connections, synchronicities. You have become a divine hologram, dear!" exclaimed Marc enthusiastically.

"That is what the man from Nazareth was, isn't it? Thomas tested his tangibility, others saw him appearing, and disappearing. And the workers in the vineyard! One still laboured while the other one was taken away. Got it!"

Marc was happy to bring the message to Maika and help her understand her position.

"You had to descend to Hell; you had to root yourself deeply through the psychological pain you endured. Only your children, your dearest to your heart, could successfully crucify you. No one else had the same power over you. Now, you are facing another challenge before you reach to your Freedom" concluded Marc.

"Father, forgive them, for they do not know what they're doing …." dawned at Maika. "You know what? It is really sinking in now. Everything makes sense! I had moments when I thought that maybe, sometimes, somewhere we had unresolved serious issues, but it could not possibly match the vengeance as it happened, if that was the case."

"Maika, can you forgive your children for what they have done?"

"In gratitude for my graduation, absolutely! They just played their role, didn't they? They did what they came for into my life."

"What else was accomplished through this?" asked Maika's mentor, waiting for her own collaboration. "Do you miss your children?"

"No, Marc, I am detached now. I am detached for my own sake. If I considered myself a victim, I'd be sucked right out. This I learned very quickly. One weak moment of the victim attitude gives power to the oppressor. Abuses are a form of vampirism." Maika was truthful with herself. Though she was crushed and desperate when events were fresh, she didn't perceive herself as a victim. She looked into causes that were temporarily beyond her comprehension.

"You can also detach very effectively by looking at everything beyond the level of duality. At that level, the genuine understanding and compassion are possible. You are capable of that, Maika," expanded Marc. "See the wholeness and embrace duality as a perfect schoolroom for us all. Yap, we sure partake of the Fruit of the Tree of Good and Evil before we can eat the Fruit of the Tree of Life."

Marc's feedback was extremely important to Maika at this time. By then, she was able to part with her recent past, enjoy many occasions that brought her joy and peace; she was moving on. She said it herself that who ever survived these turbulent times with her as a friend, is going to move into the future along her path and will always be honoured for the loyalty and friendship granted to her. She felt blessed having friends she's had.

There were moments when Marc's intensity was unbearable. At other times, he was too much into himself. He was anxious, though, to go out dancing. He was a passionate and creative dancer and Maika reciprocated with her liveliness and mastery of timing they shared. It was a great night, she said. The day before his departure, they went out dining. The place was charming, with the lit fireplace close to their table that illuminated their faces with an intimate glow. Marc had so many subjects ready for discussion and mental transport. He also was reminding Maika to pay attention to new people who will enter her life in about two to three years. He spoke almost prophetically about the tall gentleman whom Maika would recognize and who will have a similar spiritual and cultural background.

"He will enter your life to complete you. You will complete each other. Actually," said Marc, "I'm feeling his presence."

"Come on, Marc. He is not the outsider, is he?"

"No, he is incarnated. He is waiting for your readiness. You are still hanging emotionally onto someone. It has been more than painful to you; it has been slowing you down. You have to let that go first!"

Maika thought of Frank right away. They were not seeing each other much anymore, but she still loved him, knowing that she must release him onto his own path.

"Marc, how much can you tell me about this tall man? You just started something women like to hear. The prince charming image is waiting in the future. This is the perfect remedy! Giving hope is as good as the gift itself!"

Marc was not answering. He was quiet, very quiet and his face lit up. He looked so beautiful to Maika now, his eyes were glowing with devotion and the tears ran down his cheeks.

"Marc, are you alright? What is happening?"

Suddenly, Maika felt the elevating energy all over her, her heart region was experiencing an accelerating force, as if some wheel was spinning there and generating the spiraling sweetness close to graces she had known. Now the tears of joy filled her eyes and with compliance and grateful acceptance, she too kept on breathing the enlightening essence they both were receiving. It was magical! It lasted for one minute, or more; it was an infinity touching them both.

Then Marc placed his hand onto Maika's lovingly and said, "This is the way you will feel with him. You are not ready yet. You need some time. The intensity of higher energies can cause a temporary overload on your nervous system."

"Marc, I know this feeling! I had the same happening twice to me since I've known about you. There is something going on, isn't there? You came to me with the message of my graduation, right?"

It wasn't always clear that Marc was humble, but he tried hard to be. He was aware of his gift and neither was making up his claim. Maika was certain of that. She just had never met anyone like him and yet, she met very intriguing people in her life.

The individuality, the uniqueness of us all and the encounters we attract into our lives, assist us in our faith and knowingness that there is a Plan, a specific purpose in our lives. Step by step, we ascend toward our future that is personal to each of us. Indeed, there are no shortcuts. Our will ought to resonate with the higher will. Procrastination of life's assignments leads to separation from the flow that is time and space sensitive. Acceptance, therefore, is essential for the seeker of truth on the quest of the personal "holy grail". Nervous breakdowns and neurological or psychological disorders are frequently results of one's abstention from the life's current that is fully synchronized with the wholeness. Recognition of the key choices and the key encounters is crucial to our health, our psyche and our participation in evolution.

Marc left an imprint on Maika's journey and he, just like many other messengers, became a history. He entered her existence according to the Plan. Maika and I gathered that his ability to shape shift related directly to energies that were channeled through him. At times he looked gloriously handsome and radiant, at other times he was older than his usual. He saw Maika in the same light. He was not the only one having the eyes to see. She had capacity to look very young and seldom has looked her age. The spirit shines through!

SEQUEL THREE

THE winds had shifted. It paid off to hire a senior lawyer from a reputable firm. The first hired lawyer was quite upset that Maika hired another one. She explained and he had to take it. New agreements were made. Maika was phoned about the progress.

"You will receive the entire equity. Your daughter wants to collect the piano prior to Christmas and she'll consent to the sale shortly after. It's going to happen. You can hire a realtor of your choice, you set the price and your daughter will agree. It just has to go through my office first and we'll have it signed by Eva for you."

Maika was pleased about the progress. She phoned Linda right away to thank her. Linda was pleased and encouraged Maika to let go of the piano according to Eva's wishes.

"I know you want to play Christmas carols, sing along and have Christmas the way you are used to, but honestly, I wouldn't give Eva a pleasure of seeing you upset about parting with the instrument at this time. Soon you'll be free!"

"Thanks to your assistance, Linda", confirmed Maika with gratitude.

The new era was indeed beginning. Allan came to spend a Christmas Eve with his mother. There were only a few gifts under the tree. There likely never again will be a pile of gifts she used to wrap for her large family. There was less preparation, less stress; it was more festive for her alone. She was with the one child she could trust.

The next day, on the Christmas Day some of us came over and spent a pleasant time together. Some of Maika's friends were childless, with elderly parents far away.

To my surprise, she wouldn't go anywhere for the New Year's Eve. She immersed herself in preparations for the future, collecting a material for her new web sites. Nick was the best webmaster she could find. He was glad that Maika was overcoming obstacles that held her back and was patiently providing his services at no cost. By the time Maika had her house listing in place, she had two on-line stores set up with PayPal system. This way, she could operate her potential business from almost anywhere.

The house was listed. In two weeks time, the buyer came to see it and made an acceptable offer, with the possession date for the March 31st. The house passed the inspection and all required conditions were met for successful completion of sale. On the days when weather and temperatures were favourable, Maika moved more pieces of furniture over to Allan's place. Her roommate and Frank offered manpower and vehicle for transportation. Allan was happy to see his apartment filled with his mom's furniture. He offered to store many boxes and dowry trunks full of family history in his place. I also stored a number of items for her. Everything was on schedule and her day of leaving the house was nearing. Frank disturbed her slightly by asking about the veracity of fund transactions between law firms. By now, Maika strongly disliked his concerns revolving around money and trust, but assured him that all was in good hands.

A lovely opportunity came to Maika's attention. She needed to rent something reasonable for one month till her trip to Europe to see her aging mother. A bachelor apartment she liked was available to her. After she received the remaining equity from her house, paying every debt she had, she was finally free and could spend a year without an income. On the Fool's Day, Maika became a debt free person, paid off everyone who assisted her with money, having enough left to last her for a year. First, she traveled west to see her grandson and Lucy. Passing through sunny Okanagan area, she visited with Keith and Jenny. They had the most charming place with a million dollar view. She stayed overnight and was invited to do the same on the way back. Then Maika stopped in Kelowna to visit with long time friends. Browsing through downtown, she noticed a book store called Books and Beyond. She walked in and had revived an old soul connection with the store owner. They had their birthdays on the same day, born in the same country and had same Christian names! Maika noticed a young man in the store who spoke to customers about something. She was drawn to him and asked about his service. He said that he was a psychic and tarot card reader. Maika asked her newly discovered sisterly soul about the quality of his readings. She endorsed him highly. His name was Robert and he was available for a half an hour reading. They entered a small room. Maika was fairly amused by his skilled card shuffling. She cut the cards into three groups with her left hand, as asked. Then Robert spread them in his chosen pattern and began to read.

"The estranged oldest son of yours has caused you lots of grief. He is in his darkest zone. He is trying to influence other children of yours. There is a purpose in this. You are to move to British Columbia, you know?!"

Maika responded to that with a smile. Robert continued in his reading, each time adding more cards.

"There are two homes for you in BC. You will know about the first one soon. There is a couple that will lead you to it."

"You mean a couple, like a man and wife, or a father and daughter team?"

"A couple", repeated Robert, "a very good couple, likely a married couple."

Maika thought of some elderly couple who needs a house sitting while they are away for a winter or someone who is afraid to live by themselves.

"When is this going to happen?"

"Soon! You will recognize them by the ring of fire."

"Ring of fire? What kind?" Maika was anxious to find out more.

"I don't know!" he responded in frustration. "Maybe they'll have a T-shirt with Calgary Flames logo on it. The words that come to me are not always specific. I just say what comes and when it comes. You have to make sense out of it yourself!"

"Maybe when I return from Europe on my next trip through BC this will happen", responded Maika.

"It is going to happen this week!" he said. "The other home comes in the spring. There will be lots of love. You will find a love of your life!"

Robert named a region where she'll live. He claimed that the locality resonates with her energy and that it was a place where she'll arrive at her full power. He also spoke of someone who's torn within a triangle. "He needs time to grow. His pace is slower." Maika assumed that he spoke of Frank. There was more said and it truly related to many issues in her life at this time. Not a single comment was senseless.

Maika enthusiastically shared the "message" with her lady friend she stayed with while in Kelowna. She mentioned that the Kootenay area of BC was termed as the ring of fire area with a very interesting and rich geology. Both women shared common interests.

Maika continued her trip to Vancouver where she fortunately found her grandson in his other grandparents care and had the opportunity to visit with him. He was walking now and attempted to speak and to express his affection. Maika hasn't seen him for one full year! She hoped to see him the following day, but Lucy labeled her as an unwelcome visitor and made it very clear that Maika cannot see her grandson anymore, though she accepted gifts Maika brought for him. This was another blow to her heart. Realizing how difficult and emotionally draining this bargaining would be, she chose to distance herself and wait till the ripe time. Fathers of her own children had weekly visiting rights and she has never used the children to be a subject of dispute or blackmail. She would not place her grandson into that position either. She loved them all.

It was time to leave the city and head eastward. This time Maika stayed overnight at Keith and Jenny's place. They roasted frankfurters on the fire and indulged in other delights of their own-grown pickled veggies, home made bread and beer. They had a great time. Maika was welcome to visit and sleep over at any time of need. She just loved the quiet there! Then the conversation turned to a concern over her next residence and she was asked if a cottage in woods would be an acceptable home for her.

"How far in the woods are we speaking of?"

"You know our friend Jerry has two houses on his land. The tenants in his cottage are moving out this summer. It would be a very suitable place for you. There is garden, and more. Jerry is a great guy, very skilled in trades, he hunts and fishes. He is well-educated and fun too. He'd like to have a tenant like you, I'm sure. Why don't you check it out?"

"Keith, is that Jerry who had so much misfortune in recent years?"

"Yes, that's him."

"I heard about this place two years ago and always thought that it carried too much of bad luck."

"Well, you can change that! He really is a decent person and should not live alone there." Keith didn't receive any further response from Maika. She changed the subject.

In the morning, when she was parting with her friends, she asked Keith to provide Jerry with her e-mail address and phone number. Keith suggested visiting Jerry right away before her departure, but Frank was expecting Maika in the afternoon and she really wanted to keep her appointment.

When she was about thirty kilometers on her way, suddenly, like a flash of lightening the thought entered her mind. 'My goodness, Keith and Jenny are the couple who had a temporary home for me! Their fire pit is surrounded by a slice of metallic culvert! They are the couple I'd recognize by the ring of fire!' Maika was exuberant! Robert was another messenger!

She was late for her meeting with Frank. She had to phone him and he came to her bachelor suite. He claimed that he missed her. Maika was anxious to tell him about the psychic reading and her possible future move to British Columbia. Since she met Frank, he spoke of his own plan to move to smaller town somewhere in BC one day. They had a nice evening together and the next day he visited Maika right after his work. He was stressed. Maika asked what was wrong. He wouldn't tell. She passed on it. Later on in the evening he confessed that he was meeting with a friend from work with the intention of finding out what her opinion was on his relationship with Maika. The co-worker replied that he was too good for her. Maika jumped right up from her relaxed position. "What? She doesn't know me at all! I saw her once!" Then she witnessed something she would have not expected to happen at this time. Frank released his anger by hitting the cushion with his forearm while exclaiming "You don't have the damn money!" This was a huge insult on Maika, who has paid all her debts, has never declared a bankruptcy and had skills she could take into the world. Her hand just flew against Frank's cheek. It was the beginning of the end. Furious, he wanted to leave right away. She stopped him. This was not the way to part; it would leave a trail of anger for both. She couldn't afford it. Frank promised he'll see her the next day after his work. He came and acted as if nothing had happened. He forgave her and was willing to rest it behind. On the contrary, he offered a one week holiday with his camper. They made up completely, but Maika was to be away for three months and that would test their relationship. It has been very sporadic and unstable for some time.

Jerry phoned and spoke about his place to Maika. They were getting to know each other through e-mails and sometimes talked on the phone. He invited Maika to visit after her return from Europe, to stay for a week and test the place herself, if it would suit her. She told him about 'the ring of fire' and their friends' involvement. Jerry was fascinated. She e-mailed her friends about the revelation she had right after her arrival home. She refrained from telling them about the psychic reading at the time of visit. They were good Catholics. Now she confessed. They were happy to become chosen messengers for Maika and Jerry.

Frank wanted to show Maika the Southern BC, which he admired since his childhood. He took her to Creston, Nelson and all around the Kootenay region. There were places that Maika liked, but most of communities were secluded and difficult to reach in the winter season. She couldn't imagine herself living there somewhere. She seldom felt in tune with local energy vortices. On the contrary, some places had unpleasant cold energy that she described to Frank as 'spooky'. Those were the exact places where he felt at home. She also observed the agricultural potential of the region. There was hardly any fertile land. No, Maika could not imagine herself living or settling there. Jerry lived near Salmon Arm where some estates were blessed with good soil, while other lands grew rock. Keith and Jenny owned a fertile and slightly clayish twenty acres of land. Fruit trees and grapes were successfully grown in Okanagan valley. No matter what, the Southern British Columbia offered a potential.

NEW WORLD

IT is being said that the dream we are dreaming on the first night in a new location, is prophetic. The nomadic tribes, such as gypsies, may be witnesses to this claim.

Maika left Canada for three months. She was a good traveler, but this time she'd rather stay in one location. To visit with her aging mother became a priority. She couldn't visit her for the last four years due to her practice and financial responsibility. Seeing her mom again, who's been losing weight and could not focus her attention on a short conversation about the daily simplicities of life, confirmed to Maika that she must make herself available to her mom in case of a need. Her mother would never want to go to a nursing home, being as independent as she was and appreciating privacy.

A jet lag was hard on Maika again. She just couldn't fall asleep into the dawn, hearing the birds' singing by then, the first public transit trams, the early rising neighbours starting their cars, and more of city's noises. She hoped for a couple of hours of sleep. Instead of a sleep, she had a lucid dream she described to me in detail:

"I flew out of my body above the city. I had to pay attention to avoid electric lines. I flew very fast. The speed accelerated and an incredible shift of environment took place. I landed on a forest road in the midst of spruce forest. I recognized the place. It was my 'dream forest' I visited in many other dreams. I noticed a six feet high retaining wall thickly covered by dark green ivy plants.

I thought 'Hmm, a man made in a middle of the forest!' I walked along the wall and see at my eye level a twenty inch long and four inches high a newly carved pine wood arrow with Jerry's fall name branded into it. Some letters' lines looked like pointing fingers. It all pointed in the direction I was already taking. The wall ended and I am standing by the two meter wide opening, before the ivy covered wall continued to my right. In front of me I see in the twilight a nicely groomed lawn with five or six fruit trees and behind it there was a larger fish pond. I entered this place. At my left there were two houses, both made of logs. At my right I noticed a double letter size white paper posted on the wall and I read what was printed in black on it. I think it was written in English. It was a poem, a long poem written with great sense of humour and beautifully composed in rhymes. I thought to myself 'Hmm, a place of fun, creativity and intelligence!' I looked again in a direction of the pond and noticed that there was a railing descending to the shore, which must have lined a stairway. There was a male figure, wearing a barrette with shield. He was ascending the steps. In an instant, I am waiting above the stairway on the lawn. I am only seeing a black silhouette against the twilight. I hear his voice saying, 'Coffee or tea?' He was expecting me. I thought that the kettle must be boiling and it felt like a welcome home greeting. The male figure was to pass by me, when my curiosity led me to touch his shoulder firmly and turn him around to see his face. Before me was a very attractive tall man standing, who could be in his forties. He looked over the lake, into a distance, oblivious to his surroundings. His neck long wavy pepper and salt hair, his dreamy and incredibly pure blue eyes and fair complexion gave him an identity of an idealistic visionary. He looked angelic to me. He was radiant. When I saw his face, I exclaimed 'It's you!' placing my forehead onto his heart, feeling peace. He wore blue jeans, burgundy shirt and he had a white stripe decoration on his left breast pocket."

Maika wrote me about her dream. She admitted that it was a clear guidance to consider living in Jerry's place. She knew that Jerry could not possibly be the handsome man, but rather a link. Now having so much happening, she was anxious and willing to shorten her stay, but getting to know her mother's condition, her renewed connection to friends and relatives, she decided to complete the full three months term. Frank called her weekly. It was helpful. She had only a month remaining there, when she opened up another e-mail from Frank in the Internet Café. Frank wrote that they must talk and that he would be calling the next day. Maika sensed that something unpleasant was happening. She was ready for the news, with her heart pounding when she answered Frank's call. Indeed, he was not going to wait for her another month, all courageous to give her a boot long distance on the phone. How typical of him! I answered immediately Maika's e-mail, in which she described their dialogue in detail. She was distressed and I was relieved that it was happening for her now, at last, since Frank has caused her so much pain and seldom was he loyal. Maika could not be reached by him where she was and it truly served her. Two people who are intimate are very vulnerable with each other. She was passing through her Frank-o-pause quite successfully with less emotional upheavals and hot flashes. She knew that the end was inevitable. Frank served two masters and totally neglected to serve himself.

There was no need for Maika to delay her trip to British Columbia. After her arrival she spent one night at my place and the other one at Linda's. She met with Allan, insured her car again and headed west. She felt like a frontier, exploring her future settlement.

Speaking on a phone with Jerry, she knew exactly how to get to his acreage surrounded by woods. It was a hot day, with clear sky. She liked having her car window open and breathe the fresh air. Exactly twenty five kilometers from Salmon Arm there was a turn into the forest, leading to Jerry's houses. And there he was, watering his lawn - a shorter man from the woods with a friendly disposition. He showed Maika around, introduced her to twenty chickens and their rooster, then he demonstrated the upcoming harvest of basic fruit trees and a potentially fertile garden plot. Maika inspected the rock and flower gardens, estimating the days of labour that she always enjoyed. She just loved weeding!

Jerry had supper almost ready. Potatoes were done and the lake trout, Jerry's own catch, was ready to be pan fried. It was delicious!

Then he took Maika to the cottage. It was spacious with three bedrooms, the woodstove to heat the place, a standard modern kitchen, good size bathroom and plenty of storage space in the hallway, porch and closets. Maika had a good spot for every piece of furniture she kept and finally, would purchase new mattresses for her bedroom. There were phone jacks in most of rooms and the dial-up Internet and satellite TV option was available. The view from every window was charming! She loved it! Two additional bedrooms had separate entrances. She was sure to use one for the guest room and the other one for her office. She just had to wait for present tenants to move to their newly purchased house they were now renovating.

Jerry was an early bed timer and an early riser. Maika was offered to use his upstairs third floor bedroom. She kept window open, listening to cicadas chirping and to frogs' croaking. Within seconds, she was put to deep sleep by the Mother Nature herself.

After the best sleep of her life, since her pre-school years, she descended onto the second floor to the kitchen.

Jerry's smile and wishes of 'good morning' were followed by a question,

"Coffee or tea?"

"How did you say that? Can you repeat it?" Maika asked in dismay.

Jerry seemed to like the morning word game and enthusiastically repeated,

"Coffee or tea?"

"The kettle is on the stove and the water is boiling," concluded Maika.

"How did you know that?"

Sit down. I will tell you the story. Jerry turned off the stove, sat down at the round table and willingly listened. Maika described him the dream she had the first night in her mother's home. He was fascinated!

"Do you think that I am your angel friend?" He was humble and hesitant while asking.

"No, you're not the angel!"

83

Jerry felt relieved. His range of responsibilities could remain the same. He could continue fishing, hunting, chopping the wood, care for his chickens and envy the rooster; he could resume being the way he's been his entire life.

"I just think, Jerry, that by coming here I will connect to the one in the dream. Relax; you don't have to live up to angel's virtues."

Maika had coffee with breakfast of fresh free range eggs and home made bread. Jerry took Maika on a tour through his thirteen acre land uphill and into the crown land forestry. The Salmon River valley was lovely, but lacked the open view. The Douglas fir in the area dominated over spruce and pine and a variety of deciduous trees. Jerry told her that the area was abundant in woodland animals, bears included. On the way down, Maika had a good chance of viewing two spectacular log houses of next door neighbours. After a couple more nights, Maika was certain that she'd rent the cottage when available and she would stay. Jerry was joyous about it, assuming that she'd stay for years, but she committed to only ten months.

"Ten months?! Why such a short time? Stay longer! We can improve the place and make it a great home for both of us," pleaded Jerry.

"I cannot promise a longer residence, Jerry. My mom is not well. I cannot commit to anything for some time."

This is the way it was with Maika. If she could keep her house she sold, she couldn't be with her mother at all. If she sold a half of it to Brad, she'd have to get a tenant to replace her and that might be unwelcome by others. So far, everything worked out the way it was supposed to. She was in a place of her dream, with low rent payment and some additional chores she'd do anyway. For a while, she could feel at ease, until the next life's calling. This place was like a retreat for her mind, body and soul.

THE RECIPE

WHEN Maika was done with the weeding of many flower beds, she headed east to retrieve some of her items she could store in Jerry's garage in a meanwhile. She emptied her storage space in various households of her friends one by one, making several trips back and forth, each time enjoying her new residence in between. She embodied freedom. She literally glowed with contentment. Jerry made sure that she'd be around while he went hunting to other territory. That was her first time being alone at Jerry's place, knowing that bears were harvesting prunes, leaving a fresh testimonial on the lawn each time. Jerry reminded her to be noisy when walking out to open the chicken chute in the morning. "Do not ever surprise the bear", he repeated. Bears left foot prints in the renewed flower garden, for which Maika purchased many flowers, herbs and ornamental perennials to adorn the property with colours and create more beauty.

She quite enjoyed the privacy, sun bathing nude on the elevated large patio above garages. No one could possibly see her. The warm sun rays caressed her body lovingly, creating a joyous feeling all over. It was so healthy and she deserved it! Maika has always remembered to be grateful for good things that came her way and many times she was thankful for every thing that happened in her life. She was beginning to feel a total gratitude for the past years events and the freedom she gained from it. She thanked all her children in mind and heart for releasing her into her new life.

Jerry was a skilled hunter. He brought a white tail deer and commenced with proper butchering. Maika helped. Then he went fishing for a few days to Fraser River. Maika enjoyed being alone and be a master of her own timing. When she was hanging laundry outside to dry, two lady neighbours rode their horses through the property. They greeted her and on their way back, Maika introduced herself. She got invited to a dance for the evening. She was thrilled to hear about the regular dances with live band playing country music. Not coincidently she purchased new cowboy boots and gauchos! She was ready to dance with any cowboy of the Okanagan!

The large dance hall was built of local cedars by a middle-aged rancher who was a musician at heart and wanted to provide a stage for other musicians and the country style social environment for hard working neighbours, and to attract tourists. It was an incredible place with a large dance floor in the middle, a spacious area with round hand made wooden tables and many chairs to seat about two hundred guests. Their kitchen staff served reasonably priced food and the beer tap lever seldom got a break.

Maika was introduced to other people around the table. They were mostly older people who took Sunday off from the heavy labour on the land they farmed. Other people were coming over, chatted and greeted each other. It was an environment Maika desired to revisit. She was asked to a dance. It was mostly a two-step or shuffle. The band played very well. Maika was in her element – she just loved dancing. And then she saw him. He was wearing blue jeans, was tall, had those wavy hair covering his neck and his face resembled the angelic man from her dream. To her amazement, he wore a burgundy shirt! She was restless; she needed to speak with him. Maika asked the neighbour friend at the table who he was. His name was Robin and he was a student of psychology, she said. When the dance and evening at the lodge was over, Maika walked over to him and introduced herself. He had a white stripe hemming on his shirt pocket and had clear blue eyes veiled by glasses. Maika expressed an interest in his field of study and he said that next Sunday he will tell her about it. "You're coming, aren't you?" he wanted to confirm. "Of course, I am!"

On her way out to the parking lot, she two-stepped in joy. She thanked the neighbour for inviting her. She was told that Robin was single and unattached.

As soon as Maika got home, she phoned Linda who heard her out and exclaimed,

"How do you do that? What's your recipe?"

"I don't do anything, Linda! I just go with the flow!" replied Maika. "I surrender to life's currents and try to enjoy it!"

"Honestly, Maika, you are a magnet for men! Are you going next Sunday?"

"What do you think!? Of course I am! And I also know that I am not going to have any expectations. I am cool about it. I just didn't expect it to happen this fast!" she confessed.

"Is it? Isn't your entire life rolling fast? It's like a movie!" added Linda.

"Is it?" reflected Maika. "You're right. It is a movie and I can hardly wait for the new release. I'll keep you posted, Linda."

"I sure hope so! Well, this is encouraging. Any man for me up there?" Linda was partially serious when she asked Maika.

"I'll keep an eye for you, my dear friend."

Maika phoned me right after. I was in awe. She described in detail the entire day. She didn't feel anything unusual before the evening. It was just another peaceful day. Neither was she overly excited about the encounter. She acknowledged that he was exceptionally handsome for the crowd in the lodge. Her concern revolved around the purpose of their encounter and why he was in her lucid dream.

Jerry was enchanted by Maika's story. He claimed that Maika had a better catch than him with much shorter distance to get it. She promised him that the next time she'd be visiting Lucy and the grandson in Vancouver, she'll bring him along for fishing. Jerry liked the offer very much and in turn offered to help her with one trip of moving. They were becoming friends. Maika contributed with cooking and gardening, reaping rewards of natural ingredients.

Maika left in the afternoon for the Sunday dance, anticipating her meeting with Robin. He wasn't there. She enjoyed the dance and the company of the group around the table where she sat a week ago. It was toward the evening when a tall charmer dressed in western passed through the winged entrance door. It was Robin, but this time he had a hair cut. She would have never had recognized him as the man from her dream on this day! His classes started, he said after he located Maika. He had to look groomed. Anxious, he asked why Maika was interested in the field of his studies. She introduced her interest in Jung's psychology. Robin wondered why. She replied that Carl Jung took a holistic approach, paying attention to dreams. All of a sudden, Robin quieted, transported his thoughts into the depth of his mind and gazed with his dreamy eyes into the distance, totally removed from the commotion around him. This was Maika's opportunity to observe his fine features and those incredibly crystal clear blue eyes. His face was incredibly radiant!

A minute later he asked, "Did you have a dream about me?"

She was hesitant to tell him; it was too soon and she didn't want to scare him off. The country waltz just started and she asked him to dance. They danced!

He had no idea when and how she left that evening. She wanted to keep a little treasure of her dream a secret from him for a while longer. She came to the dance on most of Sundays, but he wasn't there, until one time before Christmas. They had two dances together. He had exams and usually skipped the dance, but showed up sometimes after six, when she was already gone. Maika didn't like driving on those winding country roads in a dark. He was amicable with her the same way as he was with many other people. Maika passed him her phone number in hope that he'd call and maybe visit over holidays.

She lived in the cottage house for three months now, enjoying her own space and free time she had to catch up with Christmas correspondence and to read books she hoped to read for some time. Allan was working over holidays and could not visit her and she would not drive in winter conditions over mountains. She stayed and shared nice Christmas with Jerry. She hoped to hear from Robin. It hasn't happened. Knowing well that it takes two to tango and to be ready, she patiently waited.

Fortunately, much more has been happening in Maika's life. She had a chance to see Lucy and her grandson twice in the autumn. It was a brief visit each time, taking place outdoors in a park, but she had a chance to take pictures and visit with friends in Vancouver. Jerry was fishing in Chilliwack at that time. The garden was planted with bulbs and tubers for spring flowering, fruit was harvested, soil turned, firewood gathered and stocked for winter use and pantries were filled with sufficient supplies, just in case. The winter was longer than usual and much snow remained on the ground till February.

Maika took additional dance classes in town, through which she made new friends. Then a lovely concert was announced in papers and she desired to go. She thought of inviting Robin. She asked him at the dance, but he declined, claiming that he has to focus to complete with studies and when he is done with major exams in April, he'd like to spend some time with her and get to know her. "I was in your dream, I am in your future", he said. That surprised Maika. She didn't recall telling him about the dream. Did he know something she didn't know? Did he have a dream as well?

The news reached Maika. Her mother's condition was worsening and she needed a caregiver. Maika informed Jerry about her upcoming move. She couldn't even complete the promised ten months. He was sad about it, helped her to move her household into his house and garage and rented out the cottage to a stranger this time. Maika promised to come twice before her departure flight to tend to garden. She would hate to see it wasted.

She had time to connect to Robin. He was an idealistic thinker who needed to plant his both feet firmly on the ground. They enjoyed each other's company, but the personal relationship was excluded from the list of potentials. Maika didn't live in the region anymore and she was going to be away for a year.

Before leaving for her departure, she visited with her grandson one more time, and had a session with Allan who kept in a distant, but existing relationship with his siblings.

Maika's mother was old and weak, having difficulty recognizing people. The same applied to her daughter. It was a new realm for Maika, learning about the importance of proper brain function and close relationship it had to nutrition and tactile contact with others. Her mom's condition improved for a while and then it waned again and became progressive. A month after Christmas, Maika's mother passed away in a sleep. There were only cousins and their children left in a family. The connection to her home land was slowly untwined and another form of freedom was introduced. Maika could finally anchor herself in Western Canada and look forward to her own future, her real personal Journey according to the Plan.

Maika and I have spent many hours together to present her story as it happened. She asked to write the last chapter herself, after all, she was the author and the actor of her life from the first spark of awareness of her individualizing consciousness. In reality, she was continuously surrendering to her own Soul's guidance, the all-knowing and always available at her disposal.

OPUS MAGNUM

Do I need a quill to present you with the meaning of the Great Work?

The one who seeks, does find. The one who knocks on the door, eventually finds it open and steps across the threshold. Many overwhelming descriptions of the Opus Magnum have been preserved in words of great minds of the past. The adepts were scrutinizing in the area of Alchemy, in hope of creating spiritual gold, tormenting their minds over the recipes passed down to them by their mentors. The earnest study of philosophy and symbolism, of doctrines and wisdom of sages is helpful, but also deceitful. It also serves the ego-mind. What remains in a carnal mind as memory could be put into words, but seldom into practice. Contrary to the process of remembering, which originates in cellular memory deriving from consciousness, we can apply choices serving our highest good. Innately, we know what is good for us, what can lead us forward into our future, our next platform to evolve further and enjoy the process abundant in synchronicities and the steady confirmation of the accompanying inner peace.

The quantum leap is accessible.
"The Kingdom of Heaven is at hand."

The free will granted to a human being is about choices we make and the acceptance of consequences. The manifested events

91

in our lives are presenting themselves one by one, each of them depending on the completion of the previous one, in a linear order of time within our three-dimensional reality – our life stage. As we happen to pass from one assignment to the other, other realities are simultaneously being affected by our choices, each time altering the outcome of the events and setting up the stage for the next one. This way, we create our own future by the application of our free will and we design the next step, and its result. We are fully responsible for what is happening in our lives therefore. We have created what is! The beauty of it is in the gentleness of the process. In general, everyone is kind to one self, takes on a lighter burden or makes a choice leading to playfulness rather than hard work. As a result, in the lives of all of us, there are potentially many futures, all directly related to our choices. In our origin in creation we are equal. In our own creative process, its practice and its fruit, we can be far apart. Some see beauty in what others consider ugly. Some enjoy classical music while others feel irritated by it. The rock concert attracts greater masses than a sacred choral music performance does. What is true for one person is not true for the other. What is real to one is unreal to the other. Our perception is directly related to our level of consciousness. We each resonate with different frequency and attract exactly those corresponding frequencies with their environment. We live in our own World within other manifestations of many other Worlds, within the same space and time dimension. We stand on varied platforms and stages to act our chosen role. It is much easier to join the majority and feel accepted, but to walk the talk, therefore be true to one self, which is threatening the comfort zone of masses that live within their own predictable existence, is reserved for a chosen few. Such individuals employ their capacity to view the passing events of their own life from the point of the observer. They watch the dream they are having. An observer is like a system analyst, understanding the process and its product. He/she will attempt to perfect the process, providing a variety of choices and escapes from undesirable ones, bringing the subject back on track and providing a clear guidance to reach a desired goal. There are as many different paths as there are aspirants and their chosen future to the same destination. The intent makes the difference. It is the driving force of a dreamer, a pilgrim, adept, disciple and eventually an exemplary teacher. With each post there is a level of responsibility. There must be a constant flow of energy. Everyone becomes an instrument in his/her own merit within the great Plan. It becomes an age of service. By serving one self, one's own evolution, we are serving all life, due to the impact it has on the mass consciousness of the cosmic mind. By choices each of us makes, we determine the intensity of passing through the stations of The Way of the Cross.

"The Kingdom of Heaven is within you"

The Opus Magnum is the life work, our accomplishments in attaining higher frequencies in consciousness. It is about life's transcendence. Opus Magnum is not measured by earthly material gains, neither by social status or the degree in educational institution. If we are blessed with material or intellectual abundance and do not share it, we will empty our grail very quickly and feel the emptiness, the loneliness of the soulless being. We will attract into our lives the equal capacities and their emptiness, going through a great denial pretending to be happy and powerful. Yes, we make choices and we reap consequences. Everyone can take a first step, learning from an innocent babe whose first steps are praised. Once we reach the destination, we can proceed further and eventually master our walk. The human being is designed to evolve within the ever evolving consciousness. Falling out is the greatest rebellion against one self. It is wiser and always rewarding to go with the flow and keep awake. Whether our contribution to the Opus Magnum is miniscule or grandiose, we receive the assignment as large as we are. The Universe is kind, God is kind, Cosmic Mind is kind and our Soul is kind, contrary to Ego that is astute and manipulative to guard its own selfish interest. It is up to each one of us to discern the true from false, God from Ego, light from darkness, love from fear, constructive from destructive, evolving from decaying. Understanding the opposites is the first step, embracing them as our teacher is the second step and from there you'll be taken by your own power that comes from within into your life direction, feeling Peace. Surrounded by great forces, you will remain in the eye of the storm.

My story presented in this book is entirely true. Since that time, I have met people who went through a similar betrayal by their own children. All of us had something in common, which clearly attracted the circumstances. We all were good parents in every way possible and we completed with our parenting assignment! Our children have become independent and self-confident healthy individuals who were unconditionally loved. The child/parent relationship reached the peak of its performance and the time has come to release our children and focus on our personal life – it was time to take care of ourselves, learn to love ourselves for a change, and to play. The time of graduation has arrived and we have entered a next stage of life with its own agenda.

All of us good parents have also known those who haven't been and they often happen to have very caring children who are still trying to win love of the parent, doing anything to get the parent's attention and recognition of this basic human relationship. As long as they don't have it and don't complete with it, they will try hard to earn it. Without completion of the parent/child relationship both parties cannot move on psychologically and cannot mature. They will continue in co-dependent relationships, expecting excessive attention and constant confirmation of affection. Both parent and child are hoping for a breakthrough and the acceptance of their relationship and its fruit.

Parenting is a sensitive task. We need more than love, common sense, serviceable caring attitude and sense of responsibility. We deal with personalities, their assignments and karma, with genetics and social influences. Each child needs a unique approach. When our children become adults and leave our nest, they're in the quest of their own Self. And just like all of us, they came with homework to be done. Whether their all-knowing soul is choosing a particular parent prior to conception or not, cannot be proven. It can only be assumed. Neither can we guarantee that the assignment will be accomplished, considering the free will. No matter what, an assignment can be completed with the collective agreement of the Selves and it takes only one powerful element that will attract circumstances favourable for its inception and execution.

Assuming that my children had a choice, they chose me for their mother. They shared a daily existence with me and became a part of me from the moment of their conception. They existed within my energy field. They were marvelous children, good to each other, good to others; they learned fast, were modest and hardly demanding. I was a blessed mother. Each of them left home after their nineteenth birthday. From then on, they were in charge of their own making. They stepped out of my implicit influence that created an environment that nurtured their being-ness and sustained them spiritually, emotionally and morally. Now choosing their own environment and friends, they began to blend with another podium and its players. Their moral codes were put to test, the spiritual integrity and emotional stability entered a realm of assail to attest to their readiness and maturity required to elaborate and participate in their evolution. Another life cycle has passed and greater tests were presented to their developing minds and hearts, providing circumstances for decisive critical momentums. Their egos engaged in all kinds of luring games of its playground. Without awareness and preparation their conduct and response became genuine. They embarked on the voyage of self-discovery. They sailed into deep waters of life and its tempest challenges, making choices that determined their survival and smooth passage to their destination, while I continued to do "my thing", being who I am and aspire to become. Not a one player of cosmic drama is spared. The actors we invite and allow to share the act arrive with their own free wills and equally seek their objectives. In time, the person that left our home is no more who they used to be. They become a product of their environment and choices. More we parents are advancing in our quantum leap, our children, now adults, are distancing from us. This becomes a right time for detachment, a natural occurrence that is essential. More I leaned toward my wholeness, more I was pushing my children into the opposite direction. The law of balance within the family union works this way. We either grow together or we must part. I didn't recognize the momentum necessary for an emotional detachment. Though our contact was sporadic, I was concerned about their well-being in my thoughts. My own journey could not be stopped. I tried for a while, living in denial and immersing myself in the work and other activities. I was having fun. Time cannot be stopped. The next life cycle was nearing. I pushed into the farthest opposite direction the one who was being absorbed by temptations of this world. Ron took the initiative to do what no one desires to take on. We both created circumstances for the completion of my personal way of the cross. Ron and Eva staged the drama as it happened, involving other assisting and consenting personalities that were equally on the journey of their own self-discovery.

No one else can succeed in betraying you than your own blood and flesh. No one else gets any closer nor has an access to your deepest emotions or knows your pattern of behaviour. An outsider cannot betray you. The true betrayal comes from those you truly love and have always loved in eternity. Betrayal is an agreement, a sacred contract. With that understanding I am grateful to my children for the homage that liberated me into a life that is already surfacing before me and steering me in the direction that is beyond my dreams. There is Justice and we individually are the creators of its measure. What ever happens in our lives is a gift. How we deal with that gift is another story.

With compassion, understanding and acceptance, detachment and unconditional love, you who chose me for your mother, are forgiven, for no one else could have been as certain of my love as you have. Move on, my dear off-springs, and be truthful to your-Self. The Journey is on!

Opus Magnum is the eternal quest shared by the Creator and Creation. Only a quill made of an angel's wing could document a scroll presenting many futures ready for us to abide and redeem. Many gates to our many futures remain open.

Words of the wise Kahlil Gibran from his book The Prophet console the heart and mind:

"Your children are not your children. They are the sons and daughters of Life's longing for itself. They come through you but not from you, and though they are with you yet they belong not to you. You may give them your love but not your thoughts, for they have their own thoughts. You may house their bodies but not their soul, for their souls dwell in the house of tomorrow, which you cannot visit, not even in your dreams. You may strive to be like them, but seek not to make them like you. For life goes not backward nor tarries with yesterday."

ABOUT THE AUTHOR

Born in Czechoslovakia in 1946, Ingrid Heller grew up in Liberec in Northern Bohemia, enjoying the romantic environment of her culturally and industrially developed hometown. Her interest in nature, arts and music was nurtured since her early childhood. After the Warsaw Pact army invaded her country in August 1968, she left her beloved homeland. Since 1969 she has resided in Calgary, Alberta, Canada, where she raised her five children. She shares her residence between Calgary and southern British Columbia. She also lived in Chile for three years with her family. Brought up and educated in an atheistic society, Ingrid looked to nature and human beings for the answers to the mysteries of life. Fascinated by both the complexity and simplicity of nature's laws and human existence in their physical and spiritual expression, she eventually became a holistic practitioner, engaging in effective therapies. She is working in the area of detoxification and regeneration, sex therapy, life force management and frequency medicine.

Her book "The Divine Comedy by Beatrice", based on a true story, was published in 2001. "Footprints in the Andes", deriving from her family's personal experience during their residence in Chile, was published in 2004.

"The Wise Pussy Tales", the erotic memoirs published in 2006, is offering a peek into understanding our archetypal levels of sexuality.

"In the Quest of Paradise", also based on a true story, reveals the partnership of the conscious and subconscious mind, of the outer world and the inner world, where our life drama is staged.

For information about retreats and seminars presented by Ingrid Heller and the team, e-mail: ingridheller88@gmail.com

For deeper understanding of ourselves as co-creators of realities and our future, visit www.probablefuture.com and learn how you can personally contribute to the Creation on behalf of the Creator. E-mail odonnell@gate.net.